GOOD
CLOTHES
GUIDE

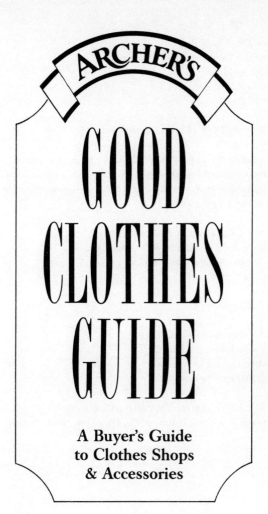

ARCHER'S

GOOD CLOTHES GUIDE

**A Buyer's Guide
to Clothes Shops
& Accessories**

EBURY PRESS LONDON

First published by Ebury Press
an imprint of the Random Century Group
Random Century House
20 Vauxhall Bridge Road
London SW1V 2SA

British Library Cataloguing in Publication Data
Archer's good clothes guide: a buyer's companion.
  1. Great Britain. Retail clothing trades
  381'.45687'0941

  ISBN 0–85223–842–8

Compiled and written by: Viv Croot
Additional research by: Cyn Martin
Designer: Mike Leaman
Illustrations: Margaret Leaman

Typeset in Bembo by Textype Typesetters, Cambridge
Printed and bound in Great Britain at The Bath Press, Bath, Avon

Disclaimer

All facts were checked for accuracy as far
as possible at the time of going to press.
The GOOD CLOTHES GUIDE cannot be held
responsible for any errors that may occur.

CONTENTS

· · · · · · · · · · ·

FOREWORD
· · · · · · · · · ·

Somebody who didn't know much once said: 'Fine feathers don't make fine birds'. I always preferred: 'Even a fairly ordinary horse with the right grooming can be a winner in its own field'.

It's taken a while but I believe the British have finally latched on to the fact that the way you look really can be the way you are. The French, the Italians, and even the Americans, have recognised it for years. But something in our reticent British nature has enslaved us to a lesser vision of who we are, far less than who we might be. And the kind of clothes we've been wearing have simply proved the point.

I don't know when things started to change, but I do know that within the last few years in places as far apart as Amersham, Abergavenny and Auchterarder I can now find clothes of a consistently high quality and design, and can see men and women who would not look out of place on the Champs Elysees or the Via Veneto. A quiet revolution has been taking place in high streets up and down Britain, and Archer's Good Clothes Guide is a long overdue addition to similar publications which have been charting the renaissance in British restaurants and hotels.

In our 'Clothes Show' road show from all corners of Britain I have been encouraged to learn that young people, in particular, have a very clear idea about the clothes they buy. And the emphasis is increasingly on quality. The truth is that quality clothing has never been in short supply in this country, what with woollens from Shetland and the Borders, tweeds and corduroys from Yorkshire and fine shoes from Northampton. The difference now is that it has also become fashionable.

The other major change that has sparked this fashion revolution is the move away from large stores to boutiques and specialist clothing shops. The trend began in London and the south, but it has now spread to virtually every city in the land. And as with major US and European cities, even the large UK stores have switched emphasis from boring racks of garments to shopping malls crammed with designer boutiques. George Davies' move into big stores, with a new range of ideas and styles and a firm boutique feel, is simply confirming the trend.

What's particularly exciting is to see how this new British fashion confidence blends with Europe's New Age Dressing for the 90s. While politicians and businessmen may squabble about what 1992 may bring, British designers like Katharine Hamnett and Paul Smith already look very much part of a European designer tradition for the 90s. Gone is the cluttered look, the shoulder pads and the sharp angles. In is a softer, less structured, more fluid but every bit as sophisticated mode of dressing.

The great international names still lead the way – Karl Lagerfeld, Donna Karan, Christian Lacroix and the rest – but no longer are they dictators. Rather they are suggestors of the way ahead. Fashion is now all about individuals choosing what they wish to wear based on how they wish to look. In the 90s we really have become too confident in our personal tastes simply to follow the dictates of the fashion gurus. And that goes for us in Britain, too.

Just as the 80s spawned the distinctive nouvelle cuisine, so the 90s have given birth to a nouvelle couture. It all comes back to individual confidence. In the Hans Andersen story nobody is confident enough to tell the King he isn't wearing any clothes. Now, we've got a city-by-city reference book to ensure that none of us – whoever we are – ever needs look undressed again.

SELINA SCOTT

INTRODUCTION
· · · · · · · · · ·

It is sad but true that the dead hand of the High Street has fallen upon the world of frock shopping; market forces are, paradoxically, driving the independent shops off the market. High Street rents are so astronomically crippling that only the megacorps can afford to stay there and now without the spice of the independents, it is a case of the bland leading the bland. This gives rise to the Croydon Effect: Croydon's glittering town centre is crammed with shops, but you could just as well be in Oxford Street or Gateshead: same multiples, same clothes, safe but dull: send in the clones.

It is the aim of the GOOD CLOTHES GUIDE to prise up some of the fingers of this dead hand. To this end, we have looked throughout the country for independent shops (or very small chains) that offer a different style and service. In these individually owned shops, you find a strong editorial grip on the fashion ranges: these people really know their customer profile, and can use this knowledge not only to tailor their stock to suit demand but also to educate their customers' fashion palate, introducing them to new looks and tactfully weaning them off old but unsuitable favourites. All these shops have regular customers, and they trump the High Street again and again with a card it cannot produce: service. After all, who can relate to a cash point? Or to the pretty, vacant staff of the fashion multiples?

Independents offer advice and dialogue; they rehumanize clothes shopping, make it fun again. It is no surprise that the shops within commuter distance of London are mopping up disaffected customers brutalized by the Big City shopping experience.

The GOOD CLOTHES GUIDE covers a wide range of shops: most sell fashionable day wear, but some specialize: accessories, hats, shoes, costume jewellery, knitwear, lingerie, swimwear, shoes, party dresses, made to measure, dress hire, antique and period clothes and special sizes (big and small). You can find out who are the most approachable top line designers, where to go for the best clothes markets, where new young fashion graduates are showing: also fun things like which Oxfam Shop the Princess of Wales has been to, where to buy a kilt even if you don't merit a tartan, where to hire a gorilla suit, where to buy lace blouses in a dungeon.

Most of the shops buy in the ranges, but the GUIDE also covers independent own label shops, from the newly hatched fashion grads to established but approachable designers such as Bruce Oldfield and Margaret Howell. Remember that it is often an education in itself to look at a top notch, die-for-it designer range displayed in its entirety. It will teach you what styles to look out for and brace you to go home and fiercely edit your existing wardrobe.

The philosophy of the GOOD CLOTHES GUIDE necessarily limits the number of big shops and massive chains covered: most department stores buy centrally (a variation of the Croydon Effect), but we single out the best of the big guns: those who have a strong fashion input, or an individual outlook. There is also a listing of the independent fashion chainlets – not High Street multiples, but small independent chains whose modest expansion allows them to deliver dash for a little less cash.

The small Mail Order section does not cover the brick-thick tomes of the department-store-in-a-book school of shopping by post, but a selection of small operations offering a specialized service. Finally, the Design Directory pulls it all together, with an alphabetical listing of every shop in the book combined with a category index so that you can find where to buy jewellery, for example (not only jewellery shops sell jewellery these days).

Naturally prices vary, from market stall to a remortgage. And after all, what is one person's reasonable is another's astronomical. While some prices are indicated in the book, obviously they will soon become amusingly obsolete. In the main we have followed a rough ascending scale: cheap (up to £50.00); affordable (up to £100.00); acceptable (up to £150.00); expensive (up to £200.00); and very expensive (up to £300.00). After that you are into megarich or gross indulgence. However, many shops offer their own credit schemes to help you spread the load.

The GOOD CLOTHES GUIDE is for (and by) real women; many of the entries were nominations made by women up and down the country who had found a shop they felt relaxed in, which could deliver their individual look. Much of the follow up research was done by real women with real jobs:

barristers, teachers, artists, nurses, students, accountants, managing directors, designers; some married, some single, some mothers, all of them trying to combine holding down a demanding job with running their own domestic unit.

Naturally, not every shop in the country is included; doubtless we have missed some. If you think we have, fill in the nomination form at the end of the book, and tell us about it.

THE ARCHER'S AWARDS

• • • • • • • • • •

Although every shop in this book is, by nature of its inclusion, a winner, the Archer's Awards which you will see throughout the book have been given (after much hard deliberation) to those shops which offer a little extra something – even more intriguing labels, even more diverting decor, even better service. From these 100 winners, nine regional winners will be selected (after even harder deliberation).

THE NORTH

· · · · · · · · · ·

CHESHIRE, COUNTY DURHAM, CLEVELAND, GREATER MANCHESTER, LANCASHIRE, TYNE & WEAR, YORKSHIRE

Huge amounts of fashion sense in the North. Go to Altrincham (or anywhere in Cheshire) for grown up clothes, Harrogate and Ilkley for megarich chic, Leeds for cutting edge designerdom, Manchester for the big city look, Newcastle for creative dressing, York for individualism.

CHESHIRE

ALDERLEY EDGE

**ANN BARNES
INTERNATIONAL
FASHION
41 London Road
Alderley Edge**
0625 583539

Open: 9.00 to 5.30 Mon. to Sat.
Credit Cards: Access, American
Express, Diners Club, Visa

A regular clientele of professional
women (25+) browse through two
floors of well stocked chic in sizes 8
to 24, ranging from affordable
upwards. Four private changing
rooms, alterations and mail order
when requested. Ann Barnes is
admirably discreet about which
labels she sells; you will just have to
go there and see for yourself...

CHESTER

**LISA STIRLING
21 Bridge Street
Chester**
0244 324120

Open: 9.00 to 5.30 Mon. to Fri; 9.00
to 6.00 Sat.
Credit Cards: Access, American
Express, Diners Club, Visa

A slightly lower profile branch of
the Manchester LISA STIRLING,
selling less demanding wear:
MaxMara, Mondi, L'Estelle, Betty
Barclay, OuiSet.

**ZIGZAG
5 Bridge Street
Chester**
0244 45212

Open: 9.00 to 5.30 Mon. to Sat.
Credit Cards: Access, American
Express, Visa

Smart casual separates from the
SAMUEL COOPER range (see
WILMSLOW). Sizes 10 to 16;
excellent hardworking clothes at
sensible prices. Branches also in
ALTRINCHAM, NOTTINGHAM and
WILMSLOW.

Lingerie

**CHANTILLY
3 Godstall Lane
Chester**
0244 314682

Open: 10.00 to 5.00 Mon. to Sat.
Credit Cards: Access, American
Express, Diners Club, Visa

Lou, Lejaby, Chantelle, Jenny
Dubell bras, briefs and slips (32a to
44e sizes; personal bra fitting
available); Louis Feraud, Kallist,
Sally Poppy and Rosch nightwear
(sizes 10 to 22); Slix and Gideon
Oberson swimwear (sizes 10 to 24).

NANTWICH

REFLECTIONS
38 Hospital Street
Nantwich CW5 5RP
0270 625218

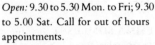

Open: 9.30 to 5.30 Mon. to Fri; 9.30
to 5.00 Sat. Call for out of hours
appointments.
Credit Cards: Access, American
Express, Diners Club, Visa

Easy parking

Beautiful old shop replete with
blackened oak beams in the
Cheshire style. Inside, it is soft and
pretty and full of all the labels to die
for: Arabella Pollen, Margaret
Howell, Ginochietti, Jean Muir
Studio, Joseph Tricot; also Byblos,
Penny Black, MaxMara, Fenn,
Wright & Manson. Adored by busy
working women, who take
advantage of Barbara Cupe's
excellent wardrobe planning
service and out of hours
appointments. Sizes 10 to 16; be
prepared to spend wisely and well.

....

WILMSLOW

SAMUEL COOPER
Rex Buildings
Wilmslow
0625 524394

Open: 9.00 to 5.30 Mon. to Sat;
9.00 to 5.00 Wed.
Credit Cards: Access, American
Express, Visa

Parking in front, paid car park at
rear

Pink and grey decor and three
floors of spaciously displayed
clothes; 10 staff to help you.
Cooper's is a popular shop which
sells almost everything you can
wear except lingerie; very good
continental shoes and bags, and an
excellent range of interesting
French party/evening wear. Lots of
changing rooms, wardrobe
planning/colour analysis and
alteration service. Sizes are 8 to 20
(not in all ranges); prices from
affordable to expensive – up to
£1000.00 for some evening wear.

As well as carrying some fairly
heavy duty lines (KL, Byblos)
Cooper's have their own label
Exquisit. This is a collection of
specially dyed colour coordinated
separates and accessories (six
colours a season) which can be
mixed and matched to build a look
that appears much more expensive
than it actually is. These separates
are also available in the small chain
of subsidiaries called ZIGZAG; see
ALTRINCHAM, CHESTER,
NOTTINGHAM and WILMSLOW.

....

HOOPERS OF WILMSLOW LIMITED
Alderley Road
Wilmslow
0625 525381

Open: 9.15 to 5.30 Mon. to Sat.
Credit Cards: Access, American Express, Diners Club, Visa; Hoopers own card

The northern outpost of the fast-growing Hoopers chain of fashion-dedicated department stores. There are also Hoopers in CHELTENHAM, CHICHESTER, COLCHESTER, TORQUAY, TUNBRIDGE WELLS; See also Dukes of EXETER.

SILK ROUTE
····
Buy your silk on the worm, as it were, from a tiny shop at the corner of a working silk mill (Brocklehurst Mill). Silk dupion at £8.50 a metre, patterned silks £7.95; sample off-cuts big enough for scarves and opulent patchwork; there's even a *free* box full of usable scraps. Small selection of Chinese silk dresses, blouses; delicious real Macclesfield silk undies – camisoles, slips etc; lots of ties, handkerchiefs, purses, etc in classical silk paisley. Although you cannot see this mill in action, they will direct you to Paradise Mill, a heritage industrial museum not far away, if you want to indulge in Victorian values.
····
Brocklehurst Fabrics
Fence Avenue, Macclesfield
0625 22214
Open: 10.00 to 1.00 and 2.00 to 5.00 Tue., Thurs. and Fri; 10.00 to 10.00 Wed. and Sat; closed Mon.
····

EMMA SOMERSET
41 Alderley Road
Wilmslow
0625 523043

Open: 9.30 to 5.30 Mon. to Sat.
Credit Cards: Access, American Express, Diners Club, Visa

EMMA SOMERSET is part of the FRENCH DRESSING group, selling the same range of good mid label eurodesigner clothes suitable for the professional woman. See page 19.

ZIGZAG
16 Water Lane
Wilmslow
0625 536825

Open: 9.00 to 5.30 Mon. to Sat.
Credit Cards: Access, American Express, Visa

Smart casual separates from the SAMUEL COOPER range (see above). Sizes 10 to 16; excellent hardworking clothes at sensible prices. Branches also in ALTRINCHAM, CHESTER and NOTTINGHAM.

CLEVELAND

MIDDLESBOROUGH

**TUNNEL DESIGNER
CENTRE
17 Lindthorpe Road,
Middlesborough**
0642 243567

Open: 9.30 to 5.30 Mon. to Sat; late
(7.00) Thurs.
Credit Cards: Access, Visa

The southern branch of great
young Newcastle house party/
fashion party which is cleaning up
among the streetwise groovers of
Cleveland.
    See NEWCASTLE entry for details.

....

COUNTY DURHAM

DURHAM

**DESIGNER
3 New Elvet
Durham**
091 3847374

Open: 9.00 to 5.30 Mon. to Sat.
Credit Cards: Access, American
Express, Diners Club, Visa

Small and chic shop in pink and
grey livery (matching bags).
Thoughtful selection of labels –
Louis Feraud, Cerutti 1881, Jobis,
Agnes B in sizes 8 to 16. Prices
range from affordable to expensive.

....

GREATER MANCHESTER

ALTRINCHAM

**BLANCHE OF
ALTRINCHAM
61 Stamford New Road
Altrincham**
061 928 0791

Open: 9.00 to 5.30 Mon. to Sat.
Credit Cards: Access, American
Express, Visa

Well established, elegant shop
catering to the stylish of all ages.
Excellent range of mid to upper
price smart daywear, casuals, knits,
accessories and evening wear.
Emphasis on French and German
design: MaxMara, Marella, Bleu
Blanc Rouge, Dejac. Sizes 8 to 14,
alterations available. There is
another Blanche of Altrincham in
HANLEY Stoke on Trent.

....

**FRENCH DRESSING
104 George Street
Altrincham**
061 941 6515

Open: 9.30 to 5.30 Mon. to Sat.
Credit Cards: Access, American
Express, Diners Club, Visa

Part of the FRENCH DRESSING/
EMMA SOMERSET chain. See page
19.

....

ROSY & CO
16 George Street
Altrincham WA14 1RF
061 941 1066

Open: 9.00 to 5.30 Mon. to Sat.
Evening appointments can be
made.
Credit Cards: Access, Visa; own
budget account

Modern, elegant silver grey decor
on two floors. Excellent range of
German and Italian labels
(including Escada, Mariella Burani,
Ginochietti, Moschino, Laurel,
Bitte, Codice, Harry Who) in sizes
8 to 16. Swimwear from Gottex
and Slix. Regular customers are
well looked after: wardrobe
planning, free alterations, sales
previews and a questionnaire to
keep tabs on favourite labels.

....

ZIGZAG
100 Stamford New Road
Altrincham
061 941 6143

Open: 9.00 to 5.30 Mon. to Sat.
Credit Cards: Access, American
Express, Visa

Smart casual co-ordinated separates
from the SAMUEL COOPER range
(see WILMSLOW). Sizes 10 to 16;
excellent hardworking clothes at
sensible prices. Branches also in
CHESTER, WILMSLOW and
NOTTINGHAM.

....

MANCHESTER

AKIMBO
First Floor
Royal Exchange Shopping
Centre
Manchester
061 832 5608

Open: 9.30 to 5.30 Mon. to Fri; 9.00
to 5.30 Sat.
Credit Cards: Access, American
Express, Visa; own account card in
the offing

A little bit of South Molton Street
in Manchester; stylish wood and
metal decor houses hardcore chic
labels: Joseph (Pour la Ville and
Tricot), O for Ozbek, Ghost,
Karen Boyd, Helen Storey, figure
hugging lycra from Val Piriou and
clothes from Spanish label Roser
Marcé. Cutler & Gross sunglasses.
An essential shop for 25+ working
women, sizes 8 to 14. Get on the
mailing list.

....

BETTY BARCLAY SHOP
9 Police Street
Manchester
061 834 0607

Open: 9.30 to 5.30 Mon. to Sat.
Credit Cards: Access, American
Express, Diners Club, Visa

The first stand-alone shop for this
young German range, suitably
slotted into what is currently
Manchester's hottest street. Part of
the FRENCH DRESSING empire (see
page 19).

....

NICOLE FARHI
6 Market Street
Manchester
061 835 1727

Open: 10.00 to 6.00 Mon. to Sat.
Credit Cards: Access, American
Express, Visa; Nicole Farhi White
Card

Do not be fooled; this is in fact a
French Connection shop, which
houses a small Nicole Farhi shop on
its upper floor. See LONDON for
more details .

REACTION PREMIERE
ACADEMY
15 Police Street
Manchester M2 7LQ
061 834 7307

Open: 9.30 to 6.00 Mon. to Sat.
Credit Cards: Access, American
Express, Diners Club, Visa

Small jolly shop in Manchester's
most desirable shopping street.
Cool marble decor and diverting
black plastic shower curtains in the
changing rooms – a bit like
undressing in a bin liner, but your
eye will be cheered by the window
display of genuine bakelite
telephones, all of which are for
sale...
  Labels are ultra cred. but very
wearable: Soap Studio, Ally
Capellino, WilliWear, Sara
Sturgeon, Wash House. Sizes 8 to
14, plus a selection of hats and belts.

EMMA SOMERSET
5 Police Street
Manchester
061 834 2345

Open: 9.30 to 5.30 Mon. to Sat.
Credit Cards: Access, American
Express, Diners Club, Visa

EMMA SOMERSET is part of the
FRENCH DRESSING group, selling
the same range of good mid label
eurodesigner clothes suitable for
the professional woman. See
below.

FRENCH DRESSING
····
There are seven shops in the
French Dressing
group which spans the
Pennines: three of them are
known as EMMA SOMERSET. All
the shops provide a good solid
range of mid-label European
fashion in sizes 8 to 18,
selected for well-heeled women
of thirtysomething.
Labels include Mondi, Fink,
Betty Barclay, Yarell,
and stimulating swimwear
from Ken Done.
The BETTY BARCLAY shop
in Manchester (see page 18) is
part of this group. Panache are
the house shoes.
····

SARA
The Gardens
St Ann's Square
Manchester
061 834 6614

Open: 9.30 to 5.30 Mon. to Sat;
late (7.00) Thurs.
Credit Cards: Access, American
Express, Diners Club, Visa;
Hewletts/Sara card for personal
option account

Part of the elegant HEWLETTS group
(see pages 31) from over the
Pennines. Two floors with the
same elegance and same helpful
staff and good service.
    See also LABELS FOR LESS in
Harrogate.

....

LISA STIRLING
19 St Ann's Street
Manchester
061 832 5200

Open: 9.00 to 5.30 Mon. to Fri; 9.00
to 6.00 Sat.
Credit Cards: Access, American
Express, Diners Club, Visa

Very high chic in Manchester:
Ozbek, Genny, Moschino, Azagari
and some discreetly exclusive
numbers. Also MaxMara and
Byblos. Well chosen jewellery and
scarves to accessorize. Sizes 10 to
14/16, prices from almost
affordable upwards.
    Also in CHESTER.

....

Hats

CLOTH HEADS and
SLUMSKULLS
Manchester Crafts Centre
17 Oak Street
Smithfield
Manchester
061 833 0122

Open: 10.00 to 5.30 Mon. to Sat.
(Occasionally close for lunch, but
they will leave a note on the door.)

Fiona Handley and Caryn Simpson
share a 'headwear' workshop
upstairs in the Manchester Craft
Centre (once a glorious fish
market) but produce distinctively
different results. Handley's hats are
pleated, embroidered one-offs,
built up from multi coloured
segments of hand-dyed cotton and
silk. She will make to order at a
remarkably good price (starts at
£25.00). Simpson's designs are
noticably more wacky – 'leopard
skin' pill boxes , huge floppy velvet
caps, brocade extravaganzas – and
look great on the young and
carefree. Prices start at £21.00.

....

Lingerie

FEMME
8 St Ann's Arcade
St Ann's Square
Manchester M2 7HS
061 832 2193

Open: 10.00 to 5.30 Mon. to Fri;
10.00 to 5.00 Sat.
Credit Cards: Access, Visa

Wonderfully feminine shop in dove
grey and pink; all lingerie displayed
on lovely fat satin hangers: Lou, La
Perla, Hanro etc; bras from 32 to
40, cup sizes a to dd. Towelling
gowns (Louis Feraud) and
gorgeous nighties (Lux Lux,
Barbizone, La Perla, Romantic
Nights) size 10 to 18. Free gift
wrapping service all year round
(chaps take note). Also stock La
Perla fragrances.

Made to Order

THE DRESSING ROOM
6 St Ann's Arcade
St Ann's Square
Manchester M2 7HS
061 833 2784

Open: 10.00 to 5.00 Mon. to Sat.
Credit Cards: Access, Visa

Designer Joanne Brooks and her
partner set up The Dressing Room
18 months ago to provide
mouthwatering ball gowns and
ravishing party frocks at extremely
reasonable prices. They make all
their own dresses (label: The
Dressing Room) and a silk or velvet

number will set you back an
affordable £350.00 or so. They will
design and make to order (allow
about two weeks) and also
undertake wedding commissions,
although this will take longer.

You can also hire one of their
confections: average price is
£60.00.

Shoes

CRISPINS
Royal Exchange Shopping
Centre
St Ann's Square
Manchester M2 7DB
061 833 0022

Open: 9.30 to 5.30 Mon. to Sat.
Credit Cards: Access, American
Express, Diners Club, Select, Visa

A branch of the LONDON Crispins.
Excellent for ultra narrow fittings
(AAA, AA, although not available
in every line) sizes 4 to 7; AA in
sizes 8 to 11; B and C in all sizes.

Crispins by Post is run from this
branch (see page 155).

OLDHAM

ELIZABETH GRAY
120 Union Street
Oldham
061 624 2716

Open: 9.00 to 5.30 Mon. to Sat.
Credit Cards: Access, American
Express, Diners Club, Visa; own
budget account available

Easy parking

A large shop, with three floors
carrying a good range of mid-price
German labels; also OuiSet, Mexx
and Mondi. Alterations service.
You can hire a hat here: a £70.00(ish)
hat for that one special occasion will
cost you about £12.00 to rent.

....

STOCKPORT

ANGELA BEER
INTERNATIONAL
FASHIONS
Woodford Road
Bramhall
Stockport
061 439 2630/9783/7740

Open: 9.30 to 5.30 Mon. to Sat.
Credit Cards: Access, American
Express, Diners Club, Visa

Mecca for professional women
(size 8 to 16) prepared to invest in
dressing. Spacious two floor shop
owned and run by a husband and
wife team who have recently
celebrated 10 years of success. The
flair and knowledge of large staff
(20) guide customers through the
label maze – including Betty

Barclay, Crisca, Feraud, Fink,
Laurel, Mansfield, and Mondi,
Escada and Basler shops. Lots of
changing rooms, coffee offered
while you make a decision, and
settees for those who merely stand
and wait. Alteration service
available.

....

HELEN WINTERSON LTD
6 Market Street
Marple
Stockport SK6 7AD
061 427 2245

Open: 9.00 to 5.30 Mon. to Sat;
closes 1.00 Wed.
Credit Cards: own account system

Classic green and gold decor is the
background to daywear from Louis
Feraud, Mondi, Yarrell, Le Truc,
Laurel and other German labels.
Evening wear from Frank Usher.
Sizes 8 to 24; unobtrusive personal
service a speciality. Alteration
service available.

....

HUMBERSIDE

BEVERLEY

SILKS
38 North Bar Within
Beverley
0482 860777

Open: 9.00 to 5.30 Mon. to Sat.
Credit Cards: Access, Visa

Rather upmarket establishment for the 35+ achiever: top class diffusion KL, Bruce Oldfield 1992, and strong range of eurowear: Marella, Strenesse, Bitte, Basler. Prices thus range from affordable to expensive.

A couple of cat walks away (well, 50 yards for the practically minded) there is a second SILKS, at 1 St Mary Court, North Bar Within.

Shoes

CIEL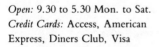
St Mary's Court
North Bar Within
Beverley
0482 860607

Open: 9.30 to 5.30 Mon. to Sat.
Credit Cards: Access, American Express, Diners Club, Visa

Smallish shop in the continental style, crammed with lovely shoes and boots from Italy, Germany and Spain. A great antidote to High Street Clone syndrome. Excellent range of party shoes, all the result of astute buying by owner Clare Law.

If you like Kurt Geiger and Russell and Bromley style, you can get it here with less damage to your wallet... sizes 35½ to 40½.

They also sell Wolford hosiery, and terrific jewellery from Flash Harry and Angie Gooderham.

HULL

VIVIENNE SMITH
SIMPLY CLOTHES
20 Paragon Street
Hull
0482 210114

Open: 9.00 to 5.30 Mon. to Sat.
Credit Cards: Access, American Express, Diners Club, Visa

Own label cotton dresses, soft suits, long and short taffeta party frocks, all at sensible prices. For more details see page 29. There are also branches at BATH, BRISTOL, GUILDFORD, LEEDS, NOTTINGHAM, SHEFFIELD, WAKEFIELD and YORK.

LANCASHIRE

LYTHAM ST ANNES

POPPY
17-18 Market Square
Lytham St Annes
0253 730826

Open: 10.00 to 5.30 Mon. to Sat.
Credit Cards: Access, American
Express, Visa

The two POPPYS are now one large
countrified, relaxed shop.
Impressive array of labels cater for
most tastes and sizes. Collections
from Salmon and Green, Amuleti,
Betty Barclay, MaxMara, Marella,
Laurel (for sizes 8 to 16) segue
effortlessly into ranges from
Marina Rinaldi, Persona, Big is
Beautiful, Ara and Oliver James
(for sizes 16 to 24). Alterations
available – useful if you slip
between the two 16s.

SOUTHPORT

EMMA SOMERSET
489/491 Lord Street
Southport
0704 41333

Open: 9.30 to 5.30 Mon. to Sat.
Credit Cards: Access, American
Express, Diners Club, Visa

EMMA SOMERSET is part of the
FRENCH DRESSING group, selling
the same range of good mid-label
eurodesigner clothes. See page 19.

Knitwear

THE SWEATER SHOP
The Swan Courtyard
Clitheroe
0200 29373

Open: 9.30 to 5.30 Mon. to Sat;
9.30 to 1.00 Wed.
Credit Cards: Access, Visa

Small friendly shop stocked with
very well-priced, colourful
jumpers (£20.00 to £40.00). Much
of the stock is all wool or all cotton.
Big on patterns on a basic crew
necked shape; very strong on local
legend: Beatrix Potter and
L.S. Lowry inspired woolly scenes.
Socks, sweatshirts and blouses to
coordinate. Sizes from 8 to 16.
    Men and children also
accommodated.
    There is another branch at 38
Bridge Street, Ramsbottom,
Lancashire 0706 821129.

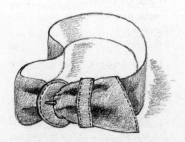

NORTHUMBERLAND

CORBRIDGE

NORMA JAMES
10–12 Middle Street
Corbridge
near Hexham NE45 5AT
0434 632214

Open: 9.30 to 5.30 Mon. to Sat.
Credit Cards: Access, Visa

Easy parking

A treat to shop in these sublime surroundings: gorgeous shop in the heart of the ancient village of Corbridge. Lots of space in a 200 year old building (authentic olde worlde fireplaces): mystified husbands can drift through the shop and out into the delightful garden to ponder the greensward, or stroll along the river to the nearby pub.

Stock is exclusively German – Basler, Fink, Helena Strasser; Philip Somerville hats. The size range (8 to 22) reflects a fascinating clientele: the shop is equally popular with the exquisitely tiny wives of Nissan executives (size 8s have to be taken in by the resident fitter) and with the more robust Northumbrian roses. Evening wear is a speciality.

The shop is run by a husband and wife team, who provide expertise, much coffee, and an annual ticket-only fashion show.

TYNE & WEAR

GATESHEAD

AMI
Unit 16
Roman Forum
MetroCentre
Gateshead
091 4601484

Open: 10.00 to 8.00 Mon. to Fri. (late night until 9.00 Thurs.); 9.00 to 6.00 Sat.
Credit Cards: Access, American Express, Diners Club, Visa

Metro Ami carries similar stock to the Jesmond branch, but is slightly cheaper. No ballgown hire. See NEWCASTLE UPON TYNE.

NEWCASTLE UPON TYNE

AUBERGINE
12 Gosforth Centre
High Street
Gosforth
Newcastle upon Tyne NE3 1GZ
091 232 5958

Open: 9.15 to 5.00 Mon. to Sat.
Credit Cards: Access, American Express, Diners Club, Visa

Clothes for the serious working woman (labels include Betty Barclay, Jobis, Basler and Bruce Oldfield 1992) at affordable prices (under £250.00) and realistic sizes. (Alterations on request).

METRO CHIC

····

Gateshead's MetroCentre is a cathedral to shopping and leisure. It's quite possible to spend whole days in here: there are shops, restaurants, funfairs, themed areas – no reason to go home really. Parking and access are easy (car parks and shop areas are colour coded). Here is the largest single storey M&S in the known universe. Fashion shopping is on the whole limited to the better chains: Hennes, Principles, Mondi, Oasis etc. AMI is one of the few independents, most of which are corralled in the Roman Forum, an elegant pillared area in the Green Quadrant on the second floor. You probably need a ball of twine tied to your car to lead you out again.

····

It is open from 10.00 to 8.00 every weekday (9.00 on Thursday) and from 9.00 to 6.00 on Saturday.

····

BREATHLESS
97 Grey Street
Newcastle upon Tyne NE6 EG
091 261 8458

Open: 9.15 to 5.30 Mon. to Fri; late (7.00) Thurs; 9.15 to 6.00 Sat.
Credit Cards: Access, American Express, Diners Club, Visa

Luxury sportswear for active fashionables (or sunbed cheats) in a cosy little shop owned by Karen Cram, wife of local hero Steve. Serious ski wear from Head, Franz Klammer, Kitex; tracksuits and fun leotards from Pineapple, Matin Bleu and others. Very friendly shop: no need to go for the burn.

AMI
23–25 Clayton Road
Jesmond
Newcastle upon Tyne
091 281 7123

Open: 9.30 to 5.30 Mon. to Fri; 9.00 to 6.00 Sat.
Credit Cards: Access, American Express, Diners Club, Visa; own account system

A largish shop in the favourite student residential *quartier* of Jesmond. Gillian Bolam runs a friendly shop, carrying a wide range of smart casuals (Laurel, Bleu Blanc Rouge, Etienne Aigner, Crisca etc), daywear, evening clothes, bags, shoes and hosiery. Services on offer include wardrobe planning, alterations, valeting and ballgown hire – for a mere £75.00 or so, you can swoosh into the party in an £800.00 Escada creation.

Ami have a sister shop in GATESHEAD's glittering MetroCentre.

JULES B
124 Grainger Street,
Newcastle upon Tyne
091 261 0646

Open: 9.30 to 5.30 Mon. to Sat; late (7.00) Thurs.
Credit Cards: Access, American Express, Visa

Lots of wood and mahogany, as befits a shipbuilding city, in this branch of Jules B selling affordable clothes for the working girl – French Connection, OuiSet, Penny Black, Fenn, Wright & Manson, sizes 8 to 14. Prices from £20.00 to £100.00+. Private changing rooms and helpful staff. Older girls may prefer the Jesmond branch.

JULES B
50–54 Acorn Road
Jesmond
Newcastle upon Tyne
091 281 7855

Open: 9.30 to 5.30 Mon. to Sat; late (7.00) Thurs.
Credit Cards: Access, American Express, Visa

Clothes for the working girl's older sister: a larger shop than the Grainger Street branch, more personal service, more prestigious labels (Nicole Farhi, Serres) added to the range and an alteration service.

PARTNERS
63 High Street
Gosforth
Newcastle upon Tyne
091 284 0406

Open: 9.30 to 5.30 Mon. to Sat.
Credit Cards: Access, Visa

A small shop in the Gosforth power dressing sector; Albert Nipon boutique, Cerruti 1881, Louis Feraud, Kemper, Portara. Sizes 8 to 14; prices match labels.

**TUNNEL DESIGNER
CENTRE
Pilgrim Street
Newcastle upon Tyne NE1 6SG**
091 232 5958

Open: 9.30 to 5.30 Mon. to Sat;
late (7.00) Thurs.
Credit Cards: Access, Visa

The Hyper Hyper of the North.
Permanent party going on in a huge
cement and chrome warehouse;
giant radiators resonate to the throb
of house music. Young, ultra
fashionable clothes for both sexes.
Own label (Tunnel) designed by
Yvonne Bryant, ex prestigious
fashion school of Newcastle Poly;
also Remote, Reissue; occasionally
take one-offs and small ranges from
fashion students, a chance to snap
up an original before its creator gets
too famous. Prices are reasonable
(from about £20.00 to £100.00);
styles for the under 35s.
     There is a smaller TUNNEL in
MIDDLESBOROUGH.

Lingerie

**PEACHES & CREAM
Earl Grey House
19–27 Market Street
Newcastle upon Tyne**
091 261 7605

Open: 9.30 to 5.30 Mon. to Sat; late
(7.00) Thurs.
Credit Cards: Access, American
Express, Visa

Rather intimidating shop, with
merchandise packed away lovingly
in tissue paper; browsing therefore
takes a bit of nerve. However, the
best place in Newcastle for
desirable and expensive La Perla
lingerie and popular with chaps
lashing out on extravagant birthday
gifts. Bra sizes range from 32 to 42,
cups b, c, d, e, ee, f and ff. They also
have nightwear and swimwear
(sizes 10 to 16) and are beginning to
branch out into upmarket clothes
(Bruce Oldfield 1992, SportMax).
Visiting theatricals (the Theatre
Royal is nearby) often drop in.

SUNDERLAND

**L.S. DEFTY LTD
24 Holmeside
Sunderland**
091 567 2531

Open: 9.15 to 5.00 Mon. to Sat.
Credit Cards: Access, American
Express, Diners Club, Visa

A good range of labels (Bruce
Oldfield 1992, Basler, Hauber,
Betty Barclay, Jobis) on two floors.
Agreeably large size range (8 to 26,
although not in all lines), own
workshops for alterations and six
attentive staff.

**MARIANNE'S FASHIONS
Front Street
Cleadon
Sunderland**
091 536 7310

Open: 9.00 to 5.30 Mon. to Sat;
closed Wed.
Credit Cards: Access, American
Express, Visa

Friendly shop run by owner Mary
Quinn; cleverly put together mid
label range means you can buy a
lined skirt for as little as £22.00 as
well as a £90.00 number; a very
respectable little outfit can be
assembled for a minimal outlay
(£40.00) or you can splash out with
up to £300.00. Jacques Vert is big
here: carries the whole range –
clothes, hats, jewellery, shoes,
belts. Also Mansfield, Peter Martin
and Cache d'Or. Sizes are 10 to 22
(J. Vert 10 to 18). Excellent on
smart, special occasion dressing
with hats (£29.00 to £90.00) to
match. A bridal branch, Mary Ann
at 47 West Street, Wallsend, Tyne
& Wear, specializes in wedding
clothes for brides, bridesmaids,
brides' mums etc.

YORKSHIRE

DONCASTER

ALICIA KITE
28 Wood Street
Doncaster DN1 3LW
0302 365131

Open: 9.30 to 5.30 Mon. to Sat.
Credit Cards: Access, American
Express, Diners Club, Visa

SIMPLY CLOTHES
····

A small group of charming
shops – 'more of a bracelet
than a chain' according to
owner Vivienne Smith – all
decorated in a soothing
shade of muted cherry and
furnished with chaises
longues and potted palms
for the indolent.
Everything is own label, as
much pure cotton as
possible, and prints are the
thing. The simple cotton
dresses and separates, soft
unstructured suits, skirts and
culottes are all designed to
take you from work to fun
with the least possible fuss.
Sizes are 10 to 16, with the
occasional 18.
The bright taffeta party
frocks (long and short) are
favourites with the college
and public school set, and
prices are equally brilliant
(start at about £40.00).
····
For shop details see
BATH, BRISTOL, GUILDFORD,
HULL, LEEDS, NOTTINGHAM,
SHEFFIELD, WAKEFIELD
and YORK.
····

Smaller than the Sheffield shop;
carries much the same stock, plus
Laurel. See SHEFFIELD.

BARNSLEY

POLLYANNA

12 Market Hill
Barnsley
0226 291665

Open: 9.00 to 5.30 Mon. to Sat.
Credit Cards: Access, American
Express, Diners Club, Visa; own
account system

Two floors of understated elegance
for the working (and earning)
grown-up woman. Expect to part
with £80.00 for starters. Owner
Rita Britton is in the shop when not
on buying trip. Downstairs is chic,
matt black and devoted to men's
wear and accessories. Upstairs for
women's wear, with a warmer
decor and welcoming atmosphere.
Every label you could want (sizes 8
to 14). Jean Muir main collection
and Studio, Bruce Oldfield,
Romeo Gigli, Genny (Gianni
Versace's diffusion line), Margaret
Howell, Moschino; hats by Patricia
Underwood; shoes by the sublime
Stephane Kelian; Liza Bruce
swimwear; exotic jewellery by
Reema Patatachi.
   Services on offer include
alterations, wardrobe planning, a
postal service and coffee while you
dither in the designer maze.

BRADFORD

HEWLETTS
141–147 Allerton Road
Bradford
0274 491311

Open: 9.00 to 5.30 Mon. to Sat; late
(8.00) Thurs.
Credit Cards: Access, American
Express, Diners Club, Visa;
Hewletts/Sara card for personal
option account

This is the SARA store revamped,
renamed and expanded. It now
carries men's and women's clothes,
from the affordable to the
expensive. Labels range from
classic Brits like Aquascutum to
eurostylists such as Betty Barclay et
al.
   The women's ranges are mainly
sizes 8 to 16, but there is the
wonderfully-named More of a
Woman department which stocks
style for the more expansive (sizes
18 to 22) – Patrizia, Frankenwalder,
Basler, Fink.

ILKLEY

MARADIDI
17 South Hawksworth Street
Ilkley LS 29 9DX
0943 600622

Open: 9.30 to 5.30 Mon. to Sat. or
by appointment
Credit Cards: Access, Visa

Car park opposite, parking outside
for 2 hours

A tiny shop, holding its own among Ilkley's big fashion guns. It's full of well chosen smart casuals – Fenn, Wright & Manson, French Connection, Diane Gilman, Hesselhoj; the speciality is simple, dateless, well-made silk separates. Sizes are 8 to 14, with the occasional 16, and prices range from very affordable (£30.00 or so) to quite expensive (£100.00 plus). Miraculously for such a tiny shop, there are two private changing rooms. Customers include local TV personalities, and all are well looked after by the two co-owners.

Incidentally, Maradidi is Swahili for precious and pretty.

....

Laurel, Jobis, Yarrell; hats from Freddy Fox.

There are two other branches, one in YORK and one in Guernsey (16 Lepollit, St Peter's Port, Guernsey C.I. 0481 714644).

....

HARROGATE

CROFTS LTD
Princes Street
Harrogate HG1 1NG
0423 561241

Open: 9.00 to 5.30 Mon. to Sat.
Credit Cards: Access, American Express, Diners Club, Visa; Crofts card

This long-established, family-run concern is affectionately known as 'the mini-Harrods' of the north. Gracious, modern luxurious shop with great emphasis on personal service (there are 18 staff for the two floors). Offers wardrobe planning, alterations in their own workroom, private changing rooms; settees and coffee provided for those who wilt. Good size and price range (10 to 24; starting price is £25.00). Labels include Escada,

THE HEWLETTS PHENOMENON

· · · ·

Fashion shopping in northern England has been revolutionized by Nick Hewlett, who has got the fashion conscious northerner well sorted. Apart from the store in Bradford (once Sara, now rechristened Hewletts), there are Sara shops in Manchester and Wakefield. Expansion culminated in 1989 with the opening of Hewletts in Harrogate, a gorgeous shop refurbished from the bones of the old House of Fraser workhorse Schofields.

· · · ·

For shop details, see HEWLETTS and SARA; also LABELS FOR LESS.

· · · ·

THE CLAIREMONT EXPERIENCE
....

Delicious clothes
for the megarich
(starting price is £250.00):
for the rest of us, the stuff that
dreams are made on...
Virginia Palm and her
daughters aim to bring the
best of Paris and the European
couture houses to their
customers.
Stratospheric label league –
Hardy Amies, Lindka Cierach
(designer of the *Duchess of
York's* wedding dress),
Balenciaga, Murray Arbeid,
Lorcan Mullany and
many others, plus exclusive
French couture.
Customers (many of whom
come from the south, most of
whom are very VIP indeed) can
be met at Leeds/Bradford
airport and chauffeured to one
of the three sumptuous
Clairemont salons,
where they sip champagne and
run their eyes over a fashion
show compiled specifically
for them...
it's a different world.
....
Clairemont salons are in
Baildon, Harrogate and Ilkley
*(next door to the
Box Tree Restaurant).*
....

HEWLETTS
28–32 James Street
Harrogate HG1 1RF
0423 504091

Open: 9.00 to 5.30 Mon. to Fri; 9.30
to 5.30 Sat.
Credit Cards: Access, American
Express, Diners Club, Visa;
Hewletts/Sara card

Luxurious flagship for the Hewletts
chain which rose in September 1989
from the ashes of the old Schofields
store. Four floors of comfortable
elegance, all limed oak, sorbet
colours and Louis XV-esque decor
– *the* place to treat yourself.
Excellent range of mid to top flight
labels (Feraud, Basler, Mondi,
Synonyme, Marella, Betty
Barclay, Roland Klein to name but
a few). Free alteration service (not
for sale clothes). A basement
restaurant and second floor coffee
shop refresh you between shopping
sessions. Menswear also sold.

....

LABELS FOR LESS
44–46 James Street
Harrogate
0423 567436

Open: 9.00 to 5.30 Mon. to Sat.
Credit Cards: Access, American
Express, Diners Club, Visa;
Hewletts/Sara card

A great idea; a branch of the
HEWLETTS empire selling
discounted designer wear from the
Harrogate shop. Of necessity,
stock changes all the time. You can
use your SARA card there.

....

HUDDERSFIELD

INTERNATIONAL FASHIONS
Standard House
Half Moon Street
Huddersfield
0484 513267

Open: 9.00 to 5.30 Mon. to Sat.
Credit Cards: Access, Visa

Wearable, affordable clothes from Jacques Vert, Yarell and other classics, spiced with Betty Barclay and Mondi. Frank Usher evening wear.

THIRTY NINE STEPS
(Part One)
9 Imperial Arcade
Huddersfield HD1 2BR
0484 543353

Open: 9.00 to 5.30 Mon. to Sat.
Credit Cards: Access, American Express, Visa

Shop full of good label daywear: Comma, Crisca, Laurel, Strenesse and Paul Costelloe's second range, Dressage. Sizes 8 to 14. Mulberry bags and accessories. Great for the Ralph-Lauren-on-a-real-budget look. For the younger set, there is THIRTY NINE STEPS (Part Two) a few doors along the arcade.

THIRTY NINE STEPS
(Part Two)
19 Imperial Arcade
Huddersfield HD1 2BR
0484 543353

Open: 9.00 to 5.30 Mon. to Sat.
Credit Cards: Access, American Express, Diners Club, Visa

Younger sister to number 9; Penny Black, BikBok, PTA and Portobello; fun range of jewellery and accessories.

LEEDS

COLLECTIONS
141 The Avenue
Allwoodley
Leeds
0532 613063

Open: 9.45 to 5.30(ish) Mon. to Sat.
Credit Cards: Access, American Express, Visa

Approachable upmarket label stable in a quiet shopping parade. Life is led at a civilized and leisurely pace: they open at quarter to ten(ish). Popular as a wardrobe for the media mesdames from Yorkshire TV as well as less public snappy dressers. Good range: Synonyme, YSL, David Fielden, Monica Chong; Marella, Crisca, Amuleti; Bellville Sassoon and Anthony Price for grander occasions.

DISCONNECTED
3 Burton Arcade
Briggate
Leeds LS1 4HS
0532 445760

Open: 9.30 to 5.30 Mon. to Sat.
Credit Cards: Access, Visa

French Connection's northern dumping ground – look for great mark downs on end of season stock (even end of previous season stock) and slow moving lines: for example, £89.00 jackets for a trifling £25.00. The eagle-eyed frockaholic may occasionally spot the odd bargain Nicole Farhi in here somewhere...

FRENCH DRESSING
31 Bond Street
Leeds
Yorkshire
0532 448515

Open: 9.30 to 5.30 Mon. to Sat.
Credit Cards: Access, American Express, Diners Club, Visa

Part of the FRENCH DRESSING/ EMMA SOMERSET chain. See page 19.

ERIKA HARRIS
43 County Arcade
Queen Victoria Street
Leeds
0532 433278

Open: 9.30 to 5.30 Mon. to Sat.
Credit Cards: Access, American Express, Visa

Erika Harris obviously spends a lot of time and trouble buying for her shop, and the result is a well edited collection of ace labels: clothes from Penny Black, Junior Gaultier, Transit, Ghost, Et Vous, Maggi Calhoun, hats from Bernstock and Spiers, and jewellery from Wright and Teague and Scooter. Fashion conscious regular customers are anything from 20 years old to fortysomething; sizes are 8 to 14, with an unusually good selection for the tiny 8s.

In late summer 1990, the shop is scheduled to move round the corner to 20 Queen Victoria Street.

LITTLE BLACK DRESS
63 Harrogate Road
Leeds 7
0532 691741

Open: 10.00 to 5.30 Mon. to Sat.
Credit Cards: Access, American Express, Diners Club, Visa

Much sass here. Small two tier shop in the high gothic mode – wrought iron rails, stone fittings, great music. It's full of mouthwatering frocks (day and evening): elegant Galliano, wonderful Bruce Oldfield, outrageous Anthony Price, sensible Nicole Farhi; ace diffusion lines (O for Ozbek, KL, Bruce Oldfield 1992); for the bold, clothes from Parisienne smartie Myrène de Prémonville and very naughty lycra clingwrap partywear from Sophie Sitbon. Amanda Pollini shoes. Sizes 8 to 14; affordable to expensive. Coffee supplied while you pose.

ROOM 7
26 King Charles Street
Leeds
0532 439950

Open: 9.30 to 5.30 Mon. to Sat.
Credit Cards: Access, American
Express, Diners Club, Visa;
personal ROOM 7 card

Easy parking

Stylish establishment carrying
upmarket labels Ginochietti,
Ozbek, Conran, Rech, MaxMara,
Moschino, Jean Muir in sizes 8 to
14. To help you spend more
money, there is knitwear from
Edina Ronay, shoes from Rech and
Butler & Wilson's distinctive
jewellery. Wardrobe planning.
Prices fit the labels.

....

VIVIENNE SMITH
SIMPLY CLOTHES
30 Land's Lane
Leeds
0532 446490

Open: 9.00 to 5.30 Mon. to Sat.
Credit Cards: Access, American
Express, Diners Club, Visa

Own label cotton dresses, soft
suits, long and short taffeta party
frocks all at sensible prices. For
more details see page 29. There are
also branches at BATH, BRISTOL,
GUILDFORD, HULL, NOTTINGHAM,
SHEFFIELD, WAKEFIELD and YORK.

....

SWANK
38/39 Harrogate Road
Harewood
Leeds
0532 886655

Open: 10.00 to 5.30 Mon. to Sat.
Credit Cards: Access, American
Express, Visa

Easy parking

Well known to the Leeds
cognoscenti, Swank supplies such
upwardly mobile labels as
Valentino, Krizia, Trixi Schober,
Byblos; evening and special
occasion wear by Bellville Sassoon,
shoes by Jourdan. Wardrobe
planning and an alteration service
available.

....

SHEFFIELD

VIVIENNE SMITH
SIMPLY CLOTHES
72 Pinstone Street
Sheffield
0742 760287

Open: 9.00 to 5.30 Mon. to Sat.
Credit Cards: Access, American
Express, Diners Club, Visa

Own label cotton dresses, soft
suits, long and short taffeta party
frocks all at sensible prices. For
more details see page 29. There are
also branches at BATH, BRISTOL,
GUILDFORD, HULL, LEEDS,
NOTTINGHAM, WAKEFIELD and
YORK.

....

ALICIA KITE

403 Eccleshall Road
Sheffield SL8 PG
0742 664016

Open: 9.30 to 5.30 Mon. to Sat.
Credit Cards: Access, American
Express, Diners Club, Visa

One of three stylish shops selling
upper echelon labels – Escada,
MaxMara, Byblos, Crisca,
Moschino, Farhi, SportMax,
Penny Black in sizes 8 to 14/16.
Expect to part with between £40.00
and £300.00 per item. Great
refreshments while you make your
calculations: wine, coffee, mineral
water, orange juice. Many regular
customers.
    Shops also in DONCASTER and
NOTTINGHAM.

....

PACE
287 Eccleshall Road
Sheffield SL8 NX
0742 664113

Open: 9.30 to 5.30 Mon. to Sat.
Credit Cards: Access, American
Express, Diners Club, Visa; own
interest free Wardrobe Account

Small, friendly shop offering an
interesting selection of labels
(including Ginochietti, Krizia,
Laurel, Best Company, Thierry
Mugler). Sizes 8 to 14: not cheap,
but jolly stylish.

....

Shoes

PANACHE
283 Eccleshall Road
Sheffield
0742 681929

Open: 9.30 to 5.30 Mon. to Sat.
Credit Cards: Access, American
Express, Diners Club, Visa

Fresh cool conservatory style shop,
all grey marble and glass. One of a
small group of six spread around
the North and Midlands; Panache
also provide the shoe input in the
FRENCH DRESSING group (see page
19).
    Shoe sizes 35½ to 41/3 to 8; labels
include Bally, Baldanini, Charles
Jourdan and their own Panache
range which are bought directly
from Italy. Also sell Enny bags.

....

YOUNG IDEAS
284 Eccleshall Road
Sheffield

Open: 9.00 to 5.30 Mon. to Sat.
Credit Cards: Access, American
Express, Diners Club, Visa

Spanky new branch of Young Ideas
fashion palace in ASHBOURNE,
Derbyshire. Sells own label
(Young Ideas) shoes (£40.00 to
£90.00) and other labels. This shop
is so new, no telephone number
was available at the time of going
to press.

....

WAKEFIELD

VIVIENNE SMITH
SIMPLY CLOTHES
54 Upper Kirkgate
Wakefield
0924 377004

Open: 9.00 to 5.30 Mon. to Sat.
Credit Cards: Access, American
Express, Diners Club, Visa

Own label cotton dresses, soft
suits, long and short taffeta party
frocks all at sensible prices. For
more details see page 29. There are
also branches at BATH, BRISTOL,
GUILDFORD, HULL, LEEDS,
NOTTINGHAM, SHEFFIELD and
YORK.

YORK

CROFTS LTD
1 Castlegate
Helmsley
York YO6 5AB
0539 70567

Open: 9.00 to 5.30 Mon to Sat.
Credit Cards: Access, American
Express, Diners Club, Visa; Crofts
card

A mini version of the north's 'mini
Harrods'. See HARROGATE.

DROOPY & BROWNS
20–21 Stonegate
York
0904 621458

Open: 10.00 to 6.00 Mon. to Fri;
9.30 to 5.30 Sat.
Credit Cards: Access, Visa

This is the original Droopy &
Browns, one of the pioneers of
pinewood country chic decor, in
the same spacious shop they started
in some 15 years ago. They've kept
their designer as well – all clothes
are their own label, and all
distinctive: well made unstructured
separates and daywear for relaxed
country weekends rather than the
hurly burly of the boardroom.
Wonderful range of yummy party
frocks and evening wear. Mostly
for the 20 to thirtysomethings (sizes
are well cut 8s to 16s) but shapes are
simple enough for those maturer in
years but still sprightly of figure.
There are also branches in BATH,
EDINBURGH and LONDON.

ELLERKER'S
25 Walmgate
York YO1 2TX
0904 654417

Open: 9.00 to 5.30 Mon. to Sat.
Credit Cards: Access, American
Express, Diners Club, Visa

Gorgeous shop, probably the
oldest in York: genuine oak beams
(inside and out) wondrous
Georgian staircase. Not 'high
fashion' but the place to go for
excellent tweeds in strong,
interesting colours, brogues, green
wellies, saddlery, proper
functioning riding clothes (the
Japes range) macs, hacking jackets,
Austrian loden capes and Viyella
shirts. Ladies clothes are upstairs:
the Georgina von Etzdorf scarves
indicate a strong grasp of essentials.

VIVIENNE SMITH
SIMPLY CLOTHES *ARCHERS*
14 Low Ousegate
York
0904 626740

Open: 9.00 to 5.30 Mon. to Sat.
Credit Cards: Access, American
Express, Diners Club, Visa

Own label cotton dresses, soft
suits, long and short taffeta party
frocks all at sensible prices. See
SIMPLY CLOTHES box (page 29).
There are also branches at BATH,
BRISTOL, GUILDFORD, HULL, LEEDS,
NOTTINGHAM, SHEFFIELD and
WAKEFIELD.

Hats

NETHERWOODS
10 Bootham
York YO3 7BL
0904 644257

Open: 9.30 to 5.30 Mon. to Fri. and
by appointment in the evening
Credit Cards: Access, American
Express, Diners Club, Visa

First and foremost a hat shop, but
rapidly diversifying. Ready to wear
and custom built hats (supply your
own fabric, or choose from their
range). Ready made hats start from
about £25.00. The hats are so
successful, and customer demand
so high, that Netherwoods have
brought in a young designer
Amanda Robinson to design
exclusive clothes to match. She will
make clothes to suit individual hats,
and also produces a small but
flexible ready to wear range which
includes some lovely floaty
chiffons, silk suits, and fresh
flowery prints. All clothes can be
adjusted to fit to perfection. Prices
vary according to material, but
£50.00 is the rough starting
point. Wedding dresses are Amanda
Robinson's speciality, and after
their moment of nuptial glory she
will transform them into
wonderful wearable evening
gowns. Sue Handley supplies
beautiful wedding headdresses to
match. Netherwoods also sell a
range of well made, all wool
knitwear in bright colours, and
meticulously detailed buttons and
fastenings.

Lingerie

LINGERS
Grape Lane
York
0904 23426

Open: 9.30 to 5.30 Mon. to Sat.
Credit Cards: Access, American
Express, Visa

Extremely full range of lingerie and
nightwear; bra sizes for great and
small, from 32aa to 46g. They do
alterations and fittings for women
who have had mastectomies.

THE MIDLANDS

· · · · · · · · · ·

DERBYSHIRE, LEICESTERSHIRE,
LINCOLNSHIRE, HEREFORD &
WORCESTER,
NOTTINGHAMSHIRE,
OXFORDSHIRE, WARWICKSHIRE,
WEST MIDLANDS

Widespread clothes choice in the
Midlands: among others, Ashbourne for
total design; Birmingham for heavy duty
glitz and power dressing; Leicester for
hot labels and experimental style;
Nottingham for smart, nonsense-free
dressers; Oxford for dreamy romantic
chic.

DERBYSHIRE

ASHBOURNE

SHOES AT YOUNG IDEAS
St John Street
Ashbourne
0335 42857

Open: 9.00 to 5.30 Mon. to Sat.
Credit Cards: Access, American
Express, Diners Club, Visa

Foot fashion at the Young Ideas
fashion 'co-op'. (see below).
Charles Jourdan, Luc Bergen, but
mainly own label shoes, carefully
selected in Italy to combine with
the clothes in the fashion shop.
Sizes 2½ to 9; prices for own label
range from £40.00 to £90.00. There
is a branch of the shoe shop in
SHEFFIELD.

YOUNG IDEAS
St John Street
Ashbourne
0335 42857

Open: 9.00 to 5.30 Mon. to Sat.
Credit Cards: Access, American
Express, Diners Club, Visa;
Wardrobe account (six months
interest free credit)

Three styleful shops in one, housed
in a splendid Edwardian Co-op
wonderfully converted: Man's
Shop, Ladies Fashions and Shoes.
Very chic well thought out
collections which harmonize with
each other: be prepared to pay
(£50.00 upwards). For women,
Unanyme, Rech, MaxMara,
Laurel, Mani, Krizia, Moschino,
Arabella Pollen, Bruce Oldfield,
Valentino, Byblos Beyond,
Bellville Sassoon, Lindka
Cierach...yum yum yum. Sizes 8
to 16. Viv Knowland hats. Shoes
are in a separate shop, but are
bought in to co-ordinate with the
clothes collection. See above.

DERBY

EMILY BRIGDEN
15 to 16 Irongate
Derby
0332 384665

Open: 9.00 to 5.30 Mon. to Sat.
Credit Cards: Access, American
Express, Diners Club, Visa

Spacious attractive two floor shop
with friendly, informed staff.
Relaxed atmosphere, plenty of
chairs and settees for waiting
friends and partners; clothes are
good clean classics – Betty Barclay,
OuiSet, Jacques Vert, Mansfield,
Aquascutum, Burberry. Shoes,
bags, lingerie, evening wear,
hosiery, hats all available, so it is
possible to build a complete look
without having to track around
town. Sizes 8 to 18 (alteration
service available) and prices start at
around £60.00.

HEREFORD & WORCESTER

HEREFORD

BLUE LEADER
3 Wide Marsh Street
Hereford
0432 278626

Open: 9.00 to 5.30 Mon. to Sat.
Credit Cards: Access, Visa

The only non cymru branch of the
Cochran chain of fun shops. Sells
Java, Monsoon, Radio, InWear,
Adini, OuiSet, Mexx, Oilily,
Fenn, Wright & Manson jolly
clothes (sizes 8 to 14). Shoes from
Anello & Davide and Zoo (3 to 8).
Bags, belts, velvet berets.

STOURBRIDGE

TUSCANI
21 Lower High Street
Stourbridge DY8 1TA
0384 393189

Open: 9.30 to 5.00 Mon. to Sat.
Credit Cards: Access, Visa

Beautiful shop in the *ancien
quartier* of Stourbridge. Small, chic
and pink, with wonderful friendly
staff who encourage browsing and
recce sessions, and make you feel
welcome even if you've just come
back from B&Q in your decorating
gear. Great labels (L'Estelle, KL,
Bleu Blanc Rouge, Dino Valiano,
Comma.) Sizes 8 to 16, and expert
alterations available.

Also have a wonderful range of
lingerie and nightwear from Jane
Woolrich. Two private changing
rooms, coffee offered and an
absolutely splendid lavatory.

WORCESTER

GEORGINA
6 Royal Arcade
Pershore
Worcester
0386 556441

Open: 9.30 to 5.30 Mon. to Sat.
Credit Cards: Access, American
Express, Diners Club, Visa

Spacious shop in a converted
coaching yard. Wearable mid-
priced (£70.00ish) French separates
from Essential (Jean Chancel) and
fun range of similar-priced Cartoon
separates from Germany; Laurel,
Gaston Jaunet, Paul Costelloe
Dressage, and next season Albert
Nipon. Shoes from Gina,
swimwear from Malizia and lovely
dressy bags from Stephanie Wood.
Sizes 10 to 14/16.

MADELEINE ANN
99a High Street
Worcester
0905 27884

Open: 9.00 to 5.30 Mon. to Sat.
Credit Cards: Access, American
Express, Diners Club, Visa

Italian chic daywear, jewellery and
bags. See SOLIHULL; also at BATH
and STRATFORD ON AVON.

LEICESTERSHIRE

LEICESTER

BAMBOO
19 and 32 Francis Street
Stoneygate
Leicester
0533 705662

Open: 10.00 to 6.00 Mon. to Sat.
Credit Cards: Access, American
Express, Diners Club, Visa

A brace of tiny shops packed to the
gunwales with splendid clothes
and knockout jewellery. Betty
Jackson, Nicole Farhi, Paul
Costelloe, Claude Bartolemy,
Blues Club, Fenn, Wright &
Manson, Best Company and Zappa
in sizes 8 to 16 (alterations possible,
though where they find the space to
do them is a mystery). Viv
Knowland hats. Jewellery from
Folli Follie and, what must be a
coup, the magical new barbarian
bodywear from Irish sculptor Slim
Barrett, the W.B. Yeats of the
jewellery world (See LONDON page
88). Very jolly staff; coffee and tea
on tap and wine at yardarm time.
Wonderful shop for the 25+ of
discernment and a reasonable
sufficiency of the folding stuff
(prices £50.00 to £500.00).

KNIGHTSBRIDGE
3 to 5 Francis Street
Leicester LE2 2BE
0533 709190

Open: 9.30 to 5.30 Mon. to Sat.
Credit Cards: Access, American
Express, Diners Club, Visa; own
interest free credit scheme

Comfortable sized shop with much
blonde wood panelling and
mirrorage, guarded benignly by
resident yorkie called Yazoo.
Splendid array of smart daywear
labels: Benny Ong Diffusion,
Bruce Oldfield 1992, Jean Muir
Studio, Bleu Blanc Rouge,
Ginochietti, Valiano, John Galliano
diffusion, Escada, Laurel, Kasper
suits; Oui co-ordinates. Also Harry
Who and George Gross. Bags and
belts, and range of jewellery. Sizes
8 to 16, and an excellent alteration
service offered if you should be less
than perfect. Extremely helpful and
obliging staff who will, by prior
arrangement, organize individual
late night shopping sprees;
browsing sprees perfectly
acceptable.

VALENTINA
20 Allandale Road
Stoneygate
Leicester
0533 702555

Open: 9.00 to 5.30 Mon. to Sat.
Credit Cards: Access, American
Express, Diners Club, Visa

Smart green and white shop selling
lots of good French and Italian
clothes: Mani, Louis Feraud,

Cerutti, Bleu Blanc Rouge; also
Bruce Oldfield 1992, Nipon
Boutique. Cornelia James gloves.
Charles Jourdan shoes. Sizes a
roomy 8 to 20, alterations available.
Good individual customer service
to help you get the look right. This
is one of a small chain of three.
Valentina is also in NOTTINGHAM
and PETERBOROUGH.

Lingerie

DIANNE ADAMS
59 Francis Street
Stoneygate
Leicester
0533 709750

Open: 9.30 to 5.30 Mon. to Sat.
Credit Cards: Access, American
Express, Diners Club, Visa

Small pink cosy shop stocking La
Perla, Lejaby, Lise Charmel,
Chantal and Huit undies. Bra sizes
30a to 42g; Nightwear from Jane
Woolrich, La Perla in wide size
range; swimwear from Rassurelle,
La Perla, Fantasy, Gideon
Oberson, sizes 30 to 42g.

LEICESTER MARKET
····
Leicester Market lies in
the centre of the city,
around the cathedral.
····
Best days are Wednesday,
Friday and Saturday.
Excellent hunting ground
for cheap clothes
– factory seconds –
some of which are great,
some naff.
····
Leicester Polytechnic has a
strong fashion and textile
department, and some of the
students sell their own design
one-offs from market stalls
here.
····
Invest in the future.
····
In the arcade off the
main market is
Frocks & Furs
source of good period clothing.
····

LINCOLNSHIRE

LOUTH

CONCEPT
11 Cornmarket
Louth
0507 602101

Open: 10.00 to 5.30 Mon. to Sat;
10.00 to 3.00 Thurs.
Credit Cards: Access, Visa

Tiny shop that contains a
wonderful collection of evening
wear from Frank Usher, Jean
Clare, Mandy Marsh, and evening
separates from Mr Ant. Also bright
fun separates from Tru, Ultima,
Spotlight, Westerlind and Mr Ant

DRESSING FOR A
GOOD CAUSE
····
Once a year, on the late
spring bank holiday at the
end of May, the redoubtable
ladies who fundraise for
Cancer Relief stage a
Designer Sale
– and we are talking
designer here
(used Diors for £50.00) – in the
ballroom of stately home
Burley on the Hill, Burley,
near Oakham.
····
It opens at 8.30 am, but be there
queuing at 7.00 am.
····
For details, contact the
organiser Carole Simmonds on
057285 717.

---

again (these are well priced between
£50.00 and £80.00). Sizes 8 to 18,
alterations available. Expect to
spend up to £400.00 on evening
wear. Helpful friendly staff.
Somehow, they also manage to
cram in a small but exclusive
selection of ski wear. In spite of
Lincolnshire's manifest low
contour count, many local
customers do a lot of serious skiing.

NOTTINGHAMSHIRE

NEWARK

JANE YOUNG
Chain Lane
Market Place
Newark
0636 703511

Open: 9.00 to 5.00 Mon. to Sat.
Credit Cards: Access, American
Express, Diners Club, Visa

The place for designer clothes north
of Watford Gap, at considerably
less than London prices.
Deceptively spacious minimal chic
shop; staff are friendly – and tactful;
Jeeves-like they take discreet stock
of the ensemble you came in with,
and pitch their advice accordingly.
(Not a good idea to go in your
boilersuit.) Prices start at £50.00
and go up. Labels include Betty
Barclay, Louis Feraud, Yarrell,
Escada etc, sizes 8 to 16. Also
knitwear and jolly accessories.
Private changing rooms, coffee
offered to regulars and an alteration

service available. Very popular shop. There is another branch in NOTTINGHAM.

NOTTINGHAM

FRENCH DRESSING
12 Flying Horse Walk
Nottingham
0602 483800

Open: 9.30 to 5.30 Mon. to Sat.
Credit Cards: Access, American Express, Diners Club, Visa

Southernmost representative of the French Dressing/Emma Somerset Group (see page 19). Rather chaotic style, with everything thrown together on three floors. Many continental labels, Panache shoes and LA Gear trainers. Fun if you like treasure-hunting.

JAMES
31 Pelham Street
Nottingham NG1 2EA
0602 472540

Open: 9.00 to 5.00 Mon. to Sat.
Credit Cards: Access, Visa

Small, friendly shop stocking a large selection of headwear from well known hatters: Philip Somerville, Peter Bettley, Genevieve Louis, Kangol, Right Impressions, Hat Studio, Della. Prices range from £10.00 to £200.00. Helpful informed staff; hats can be altered to fit, or you can order one to be made to measure. Upstairs for wedding wear.

ALICIA KITE
12 Exchange Arcade
Nottingham
0602 47808

Open: 9.30 to 5.30 Mon. to Sat.
Credit Cards: Access, American Express, Diners Club, Visa

Southern arm of the Kite empire. Large modern shop; Escada, Crisca, MaxMara, Penny Black, Byblos, Moschino, Nicole Farhi. Sizes 8 to 14/16, prices reasonable considering the labels (£40.00 to £300.00). Wine, coffee, fizzy water and juice served to dithering regulars. Other Alicia Kites in DONCASTER and SHEFFIELD.

VIVIENNE SMITH
SIMPLY CLOTHES
32 Wheelergate
Nottingham
0602 411234

Open: 9.00 to 5.30 Mon. to Sat.
Credit Cards: Access, American Express, Diners Club, Visa

Own label cotton dresses, soft suits, long and short taffeta party frocks all at sensible prices. For more details see page 29. There are also branches at BATH, BRISTOL, GUILDFORD, HULL, LEEDS, SHEFFIELD, WAKEFIELD and YORK.

MONDI
15 Flying Horse Walk
Nottingham
0602 483285

Open: 9.30 to 5.30 Mon. to Sat.
Credit Cards: Access, American
Express, Diners Club, Visa

A brilliant shop; reputedly the best
of the Mondi line (albeit by a
partisan vote); helped by the fact
that it is housed in a beautiful old
black and white building; the
interior is charming – all different
levels, with unexpected old
fireplaces, dried flowers and
revivifying bowls of pot-pourri.
Lots of seats and mags for flagging
friends – like shopping in a well
kept country inn. Wonderful
changing rooms with saucy satin
curtains. Helpful friendly staff and
a very comfortable atmosphere.
They sell, naturally, all Mondi
gear: smart daywear, glitzy
evening frocks, belts, bags and
jewellery. Don't go in if you don't
want to spend any money, you will
only distress yourself.

JANE YOUNG
21 Upper Parliament Street
Nottingham
0602 417579

Open: 9.00 to 5.00 Mon. to Sat.
Credit Cards: Access, American
Express, Diners Club, Visa

Branch of popular designer label
shop in NEWARK. Similar range and
sizing to the sister shop.

VALENTINA
11 Victoria Street
Nottingham
0602 506717

Open: 9.00 to 5.30 Mon. to Sat.
Credit Cards: Access, American
Express, Diners Club, Visa

One of the trio of smart green and
white shops majoring in Italian and
French clothes (Mani and the like).
Sizes 8 to 20. See Valentina in
LEICESTER and PETERBOROUGH.

ZIGZAG
40 Bridlesmith Gate
Nottingham

Open: 9.00 to 5.30 Mon. to Sat.
Credit Cards: Access, American
Express, Visa

Smart casual separates from the
SAMUEL COOPER range (see
WILMSLOW). Sizes 10 to 16;
excellent hardworking clothes at
sensible prices. Branches also in
ALTRINCHAM, CHESTER and
WILMSLOW.

OXFORDSHIRE

OXFORD

CAMPUS
44–45 High Street
Oxford
0865 241312

Open: 9.30 to 5.30 Mon. to Fri; 9.30
to 6.00 Sat.
Credit Cards: Access, American

Express, Diners Club, Visa; they also offer their own interest free credit scheme.

The southern ambassador of the Betty Davis Scottish Academy. Lovely clothes for girls in their prime, extremely popular with fashion conscious boffins. Gorgeous setting on the mellow curve of the High (once the most beautiful street in England) almost facing the venerable gates of Univ. Day and evening wear from Jean Muir, KL, Ginochietti, Terence Nolder; best known for excellent own label (Academy Collection) of separates, tops, suits, classic daywear, and some ballgowns featuring Betty Davis's use of tweeds and other traditional fabrics in off-beat colours. The Academy Collection hats are great fun: eccentric headwear for the brainy romantic. Sizes are 8 to 16 and alterations can be made. There are Campuses in EDINBURGH and GLASGOW.

....

DESIGNING WOMAN
31 Walton Street
Oxford
0865 513266

Open: 10.00 to 5.00 Mon. to Sat; though closing hours flexible
Credit Cards: Access, American Express, Visa

Excellent one to one service in a small(ish) but dashingly chic shop. Exciting labels: MaxMara, Synonyme, Myrène de Prémonville, KL, Sophie Sitbon, Ami Modo. Sizes 8 to 16, alteration

service; accessories from Osprey (belts), jewellery from Pellini. Prices are v. reasonable considering the service you get: £25.00 to £400.00. Media celebs like the discreet charm of shopping here. Walton Street is a little removed from central Oxford, but is gaining more ground as a shopping area as you can actually park there.

....

ANNABEL HARRISON
36 Little Clarendon Street
Oxford OX1 2HU
0865 512936

Open: 10.00 to 5.30 Mon. to Sat.
Credit Cards: Access, American Express, Visa

A branch of the chic Annabel/ Alison Harrison chain; minimal yet seductive decor, friendly and helpful staff and wonderful clothes: Mani, Arabella Pollen, Armani Jeans Collection, Georges Rech, Paul Costelloe, Nicole Farhi, Ralph Lauren, Adrienne Vittadini, Dorothée Bis, Strenesse. Hats from Viv Knowland and Siggi; gilt ridden jewellery from Chantal; belts from Osprey and J & M Davidson. These elegant clothes suit any age group who can manage the size (6/8 to 16, occasionally 18). Prices range from £5.00 (some accessories) to £600.00. There is no mail order, but they will post things to you. Spot not a few famous actresses in here (the Oxford Playhouse is nearby).

Other Alison/Annabel Harrisons in BATH, CHELTENHAM and LEAMINGTON SPA.

....

MATCH
1 Dartington House
Little Clarendon Street
Oxford
0865 514947

Open: 9.30 to 5.30 Mon. to Sat.
Credit Cards: Access, Visa

Unpretentious style at refreshing
prices (£15.00 to £100.00). Wide
range for a small shop; great
selection of very wearable,
sprightly separates: InWear,
Cartoon, Part Two, Bik Bok, Chill
Time, Sampa, PTA. Sizes 6/8 to
16. Private changing rooms. Small
selection of shoes, some lingerie
(Rosy), knitwear and pretty
handmade nightwear.

NEXT TO NOTHING
Fourth Avenue
Covered Market
Broad Street
Oxford
0865 246919

Open: 10.00 to 5.00 Mon. to Thurs;
9.30 to 5.30 Fri. and Sat.
Credit Cards: Access, American
Express, Diners Club, Visa

Shop in the wonderful Covered
Market just off the Broad. Do not
get excited, as the name does not
mean unforgettable bargains, but
describes its position adjacent to the
knitwear shop NOTHING (see
below). Even so, a great place for
lots of fun, easy to wear, agreeably
scatty clothes at reasonable prices:
T-shirts, separates, flowery frocks:
French Connection, Java, Oilily,
Triangle, Sun & Sand, Interlinks,

Naf Naf, Adini etc. T-shirts from
American company Hanes. Sizes 10
to 14, but some of the styles will fit
a 16. Straw hats too. They have a
children's department called Two
Foot Nothing.

TUMI
Little Clarendon Street
Oxford
0865 512307

Open: 9.30 to 6.00 Mon. to Sat.
Credit Cards: Access, Visa

Authentic South American
jewellery and objects; thick Latin
knits, hairy gaucho shirts, hard felt
hats from the same stable as Tucan
in BRIGHTON. Ethnic chic for a
fraction of designer prices if you
put your own look together.

Knitwear

NOTHING
Fourth Avenue
Covered Market
Broad Street
Oxford
0865 249568

Open: 10.00 to 5.00 Mon. to Wed;
10.00 to 4.00 Thurs; 9.30 to 5.15
Fri. and Sat.
Credit Cards: Access, Visa

Quite a find; large amounts of
knitwear from the UK: Maggie
White, Josephine Baker, Elizabeth
Gash, Ann Simmons etc. Not an
Italian in sight, but a delegation
from the north with a range of
bracing chunky Norwegian knits.

Sizes s, m and l for women, 38 to 46 for men. Prices begin at a pocket warming £26.95 and go on to £150.00. Also lots of ethnicy jewellery in natural materials – wood, shells, beads and so on from £2.00 to £30.00.

Lingerie

SARATOGA
115 Walton Street
Oxford OX2 6AJ
0865 310701

Open: 10.00 to 5.30 Tues. to Sat; closed all day Monday
Credit Cards: Access, American Express, Visa

Very interesting unusual lingerie shop. Clever avoidance of the pink motif; creamy walls and an exotic tented ceiling. The changing room is a luxurious boudoir. Sells La Perla of course, full range plus fragrances and bath range. Also experimenting with young English designers: Deshabillée pure silk lingerie, including beautifully made saucy garters (creamy white for everyday, blue ones for brides, red ones for a Valentine, black ones for ?); classic plain silk underwear with great french seaming and meticulous attention to stitching from Chimère; deeply luxurious top of the range silk (with real silk lace) from Sarah de Pledge in an opulent shade of rich cream (expect to pay about £120.00); equally gorgeous fine cotton lawn range from the same designer – bags of thought out style and detailing. For all labels, sizes range from 32aa to 38dd in bras; 10 to 16 everything else. Nightwear just as beguiling: knee length crisp cotton nighties, lots of demure pintucking, from Malizia (about £50.00); beautiful repro Victorian nighties from Lunn Antiques at about £40.00: all the style but none of the laundry problems. Also has jewellery from Rocks in the Butler & Wilson style. Starting price about £20.00. Extremely helpful, knowledgeable owner; everything gift wrapped when you buy it.

OXFAM, MA'AM
· · · ·
Oxfam is famous for dressing the impoverished stylish. The North Oxford branch in Summertown, which specializes in period and antique clothes and old lace, has a richer catchment area than most: one week they were able to fill their window with Mondi.
· · · ·
The Princess of Wales dropped in in February, after a local engagement.
· · · ·
Who are you to stay away.
· · · ·

Party Frocks

ANNABELINDA
6 Gloucester Street
Oxford OX1 2BN
0865 246806

Open: 9.30 to 5.30 Mon. to Sat.
Credit Cards: Access, American
Express, Diners Club, Visa

Still making mouthwatering ball
gowns and party frocks to order as
well as stocking ready to wear party
and daywear. Lots of exotic
materials to choose from. There is
an AnnaBelinda concession in
Liberty's of London, carrying the
ready to wear range and some made
to measure, but not so much choice
of fabric (you can however have
fittings in London). Naturally,
prices vary. AnnaBelinda have
been making gorgeous frocks for
20 years or so, and they are just as
wonderful as they always were.

STAFFORDSHIRE

HANLEY

BLANCHE OF
ALTRINCHAM
18 Piccadilly
Hanley
Stoke on Trent
Staffordshire
0782 284424

Open: 9.00 to 5.30 Mon. to Sat; late
(7.00) Tues.
Credit Cards: Access, American
Express, Visa

Sister shop to the Altrincham
Blanche (see page 17).

Superbly elegant shop – a little
bit of Milan (or Paris) in Hanley –
catering for a slightly younger age
group: WilliWear as well as
excellent French and Italian labels
(Marella, Balan etc). Well informed
staff who know their fashion;
clothes brought directly from
Paris. Size 8 to 14; alteration
service. Another Blanche is in the
planning pipeline – probably
Somewhere in the Midlands.

LICHFIELD

JOY ROBSON
The Precinct
Lichfield
0543 264598

Open: 9.30 to 5.30 Mon. to Fri.
Credit Cards: Access, American
Express, Diners Club, Visa

Large shop with no less than 10
changing rooms; excellent selection
of classic labels, including Jaeger.
Sizes are 8 to 18, and alterations can
be made. Prices are affordable –
£50.00 to £500.00 – and it is a very
pleasant shop to shop in, whether
you are going for the whole outfit
or merely flirting with smart
casuals. Coffee served.

STONE

SOMETHING SPECIAL
16a High Street
Stone
0785 815507

Open: 9.30 to 5.30 Mon. to Sat.
Credit Cards: Access, American
Express, Diners Club, Visa

Tiny crowded shop; a good range
of mid price eurolabels, specializing
in Mondi. Sizes from 8 to 18
(alterations possible) and prices
from £50.00 upwards. Although
the clothes are of necessity rather
squashed together, they are a
pleasure to browse through, and
staff are relaxed and helpful.

···

WARWICKSHIRE

KENILWORTH

Shoes

CORNICHE
3 Warwick House
Station Road
Kenilworth
0926 512237

Open: 9.30 to 5.00 Mon. to Sat.
Credit Cards: Access, Visa

Interesting shoe shop in
unpromising modern block. Shoes
from Pancaldi, Baldanini, Stuart
Wiseman in unusual colours:
terracotta, khaki, chestnut. Inside
the shop, the shoes are displayed in
attention grabbing colour
groupings; lots of metallics for the
summer. Printed silk occasion
shoes a speciality. Sizes 4 to 8.
Dressy, decorative bags from
Stephanie Wood, everyday bags
from Patterson. Belts and some
jewellery, glitzy hair decor.
Intriguing shop that attracts
customers from far afield.

···

LEAMINGTON SPA

GINGER
20a Regent Street
Leamington Spa CV32 5EH
0926 451386

Open: 10.00 to 5.00 Mon. to Fri;
10.00 to 6.00 Sat.
Credit Cards: Access, American
Express, Diners Club, Visa

Small, peachy shop hidden away
off the beaten track. Good mid to
upper range daywear from Crisca,
Jaunet, Bitte, Maska, Unanyme, La
Bombola, Amuleti, Marc Cain and
Portara in sizes 8 to 16 (occasional
18). Good range of Italian knitwear
and swimwear from Jerry Hall (no
you don't have to be eight feet tall
to wear it). Warm inviting
atmosphere – coffee, settees, and
flexible opening hours for regular
customers.

···

ALISON HARRISON
16 Park Street
Leamington Spa
0926 334880

Open: 9.30 to 5.30 Mon. to Sat.
Credit Cards: Access, American
Express, Visa

Newest of the Annabel/Alisons;
very elegant wearable clothes. See
BATH, CHELTENHAM, OXFORD.

STRATFORD ON AVON

MADELEINE ANN
39 Sheep Street
Stratford on Avon
0789 297229

Open: 9.00 to 5.30 Mon. to Sat.
Credit Cards: Access, American
Express, Diners Club, Visa

Italian chic daywear, jewellery and
bags. See SOLIHULL; also at BATH
and WORCESTER.

SEPTEMBER THREE
7–9 Union Street,
Stratford on Avon CV37 6QT
0789 414382

Open: 10.00 to 6.00 Mon. to Fri;
9.00 to 5.30 Sat.
Credit Cards: Access, American
Express, Diners Club, Visa

Same prestigious designer
collections as in the BIRMINGHAM
shop. Customers looked after by
very informed helpful staff. The
French green and gold decor is
repeated.

WEST MIDLANDS

BIRMINGHAM

HOUSE OF ISOBEL
13 Cannon Street
Birmingham B2 5EN
021 633 3026

Open: 9.00 to 5.30 Mon. to Sat.
Credit Cards: Access, American
Express, Diners Club, Visa

Spacious elegance for people of
wealth and taste; very upmarket
and unerringly chic: MaxMara,
Joseph, Murray Arbeid, Bellville
Sassoon, exclusive French and
Italian couture. Dale Zissman and
her team go buying personally in
Paris, Milan and Düsseldorf.
Special occasion wear and bridal
feature heavily; lots of delicious
hats. Sizes 10 to 16 and a state of the
art alterations service (four
seamstresses on hand in the
workroom). Entrancingly
expensive: start at £80.00 and go up
to £2000.00 for a really serious
ensemble. Lots of coffee supplied
while you think about it and chaises
longues and settees for wilting
chaps.

JOHNNY MALLE
11 Ethel Street
Birmingham B2 4BG
021 643 0160

Open: 10.00 to 6.00 Mon. to Sat.
Credit Cards: Access, Visa

Small, newly opened shop with the
admirable aim of selling a dashing

outfit that leaves you some change out of £100.00. Clothes aimed at the young and adventurous, with good bodies. Betty Jackson, Wet, Cocky Shed, sizes 10 to 14. Occasional one-offs from young local designers – stay ahead of the game and snap up a pre-trend trend. Great costume jewellery from Sue Askew and Hazel Atkinson.

PINKY'S
12 Warstone Mews
Warstone Lane
Hockley
Birmingham
021 236 9249

Open: 10.00 to 5.30 Mon. to Sat.
Credit Cards: Access, American Express, Diners Club, Visa

Stunning deco shop (all black, pink and chrome) in the old jewellery quarter of Birmingham, now up and coming as the old factories and warehouses are refurbished à la Glasgow. Shamelessly wonderful frocks here: Ozbek, Galliano, Moschino; also Krizia, Sara Sturgeon, Ginochietti, Extravert; ongoing turnover as new stock is bought weekly – clothes with a long shelf line are marked down regularly. Sizes 8 to 14, prices from £60.00 to astronomical. Run by Barbara Aston and her daughter in a very hands-on, friendly manner: there's a box of toys for bored tinies. They know their regulars so well that they can organize birthday and Christmas presents at the request of far-flung partners. Chaps love shopping here for their girlfriends/wives. Great favourite with rock stars: the extended family of local big band UB40 dress here, as do many other celebs. Sofa to sit on if you get blinded by stardust.

RIZZO
17 Ethel Street
New Street
Birmingham
021 643 6506

Open: 10.30 to 6.00 Mon to Fri; 10.00 to 6.00 Sat.
Credit Cards: Access, American Express, Diners Club, Visa

Small whizzy black and white shop selling men's and women's clothes. Hunting ground for young(ish) media folk: lots of Junior Gaultier plus Hamnett II, Remote and Carole Elsworth. Sizes 10 to 14. Prices £25.00 to £250.00. Very friendly staff.

THE RAG MARKET
· · · ·
Tuesday, Friday & Saturday
· · · ·
Birmingham's Rag Market is near the hideous Bullring. Here you can buy beautiful and exotic fabrics (for saris) and some good quality old clothes.
· · · ·
Excellent finds for the discerning.
· · · ·

SEPTEMBER THREE
53 Stephenson Street
Birmingham B2 4DH
021 643 7269

Open: 10.00 to 6.00 Mon. to Fri;
9.00 to 5.30 Sat; by appointment
Credit Cards: Access, American
Express, Diners Club, Visa; own
Wardrobe account

Dramatic green and gold decor,
much swagging, huge plants: the
aim is a turn of the century Parisian
salon. Two floors of designer style,
with emphasis on the Italian for the
serious dressers of the West
Midlands: Genny, Mani, Rech,
Valentino, YSL, Dior 2. Serious
prices too: £50.00 to four figures.
Sizes 8 to 14, and an alteration
service. They have all the shoes,
hats, accessories you need. Loads
of coffee ('the clothes are free, the
coffee's very expensive'), very
informed and helpful staff. Lots of
Central TV newsreaders trust their
wardrobe to September Three.
There is also a shop in STRATFORD
ON AVON.

SOLIHULL

MADELEINE ANN
45 Drury Lane
Solihull B91 3BP
021 704 9454

Open: 9.00 to 5.30 Mon. to Sat.
Credit Cards: Access, American
Express, Diners Club, Visa

The capo di tutti capi of the four
Italianesque Madeleine Ann shops.
Monochrome minimalism with
mainly Italian labels: Mani,
MaxMara, Maska, Amuleti,
Crisca, Krizia, Mimmina; also
Strenesse and Byblos Beyond.
Sizes 8 to 14, alterations available.
Bags (Caputti) and jewellery
(Pellini) reinforce the Italian theme.
Pricey but good quality. The shops
are named after their owner, and
there are more Madeleines in BATH,
STRATFORD ON AVON and
WORCESTER.

CHEAP CHIC
····
Students from the universities
(Brum and Aston) and polys go
to **Houghton's** second
hand shop in Moseley
High Street
(021 449 9953)
····
Tiny **Folio 50**, 137 Digbeth
High Street
(0221 6436266)
sells retro but new American
40s and 50s gear and lived and
loved in Levis. Distinct 50s
theming and a weeny tea room
at the back.
····

THE WEST COUNTRY

· · · · · · · · · ·

AVON, CORNWALL, DEVON, DORSET, GLOUCESTERSHIRE, SOMERSET, WILTSHIRE

The West Country is still a repository of classic country chic and traditional elegance. Go to Bath (especially Shires Yard) for timeless elegance (Bath has been fashionable since Jane Austen's day, and before); Bristol for fun clothes; Cheltenham (especially Montpellier) for total upmarket chic; Exeter for great designer bargains.

AVON

BATH

CATCH 22
22 Broad Street
Bath BA1 5NL
0225 444943

Open: 10.00 to 5.00 Tues. to Sat;
late (by appointment) Thurs; closed
Mon.
Credit Cards: Access, Diners Club,
Visa

V. friendly chic little shop, owned
and run by former model Sally
Stewart-Davis who believes that
shopping should be fun, and who
really knows her stuff. Excellent
range of personally selected
exclusive French and Italian smart
casuals. The aim is versatility: good
basics plus clever additions and
accessories for style updates and an
individual look. Sizes 10 to 14,
concentrating on the smaller end of
the scale. Prices are reasonable:
around £100.00 for a jacket. Also
exclusive French belts from Denise
Denis, wonderful costume
jewellery at prices other shops
cannot reach, and equally
bargainful hair ornaments – Liberty
style velvet alice bands at well
below Liberty price tags.
Rassurelle swimwear in the
summer. Really satisfying
shopping: rapidly becoming the
meeting place for the Bath chic and
expatriates down for the weekend.

....

DROOPY & BROWNS
21 Milsom Street
Bath
0225 463796

Open: 10.00 to 6.00 Mon. to Sat.
Credit Cards: Access, Visa; also
accept cheques for any amount, as
they have a clearing agency

Own label day and evening wear;
the same stock as in YORK. Droopy
& Browns are also in LONDON and
EDINBURGH.

....

EPISODE
5 Union Street
Bath
0225 466313

This branch of Episode is opening
after the GUIDE goes to press.
Contact London Episode (071 584
7047) for information.

Episode 2 of the new London shop
(see page 162) selling gorgeous
affordable, mellow casuals; lots of
sandwashed silk and linen in lovely
unfussy colours. Sizes 10 to 16.

....

ANNABEL HARRISON
14 Shires Yard
Milsom Street
Bath
0225 447578

Open: 9.30 to 5.30 Mon. to Sat.
Credit Cards: Access, American
Express, Diners Club, Visa

Chrome and white palace of chic
full of lovely expensive clothes:
Mani, Lauren Polo, Georges Rech,
Strenesse, Dorothée Bis; also

Nicole Farhi. If your bank balance will allow you to do more than press your nose against the window pane, you will find the staff are very helpful and well informed.

Rather confusingly, Annabel Harrison is also Alison Harrison. There are other Annabel/Alisons in CHELTENHAM, OXFORD and a new one in LEAMINGTON SPA.

....

IMAGE
19 Northumberland Place
Bath BA1 5AR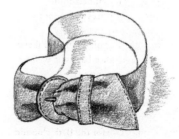
0225 461798

Open: 9.30 to 5.30 Mon. to Sat.
Credit Cards: Access, American Express, Visa; own credit scheme

Yummy shop with all the right stuff: Ginochietti, Synonyme de Georges Rech, Nouelle Roudine, shirts by Renata Nucci, clothes and knitwear by the wondrous Edina Ronay, Paul Costelloe's Dressage, Osprey belts, Georgina van Etzdorf chiffons, Ami Modo Spanish knitwear. They are also trying out a range of sprightly clothes in larger sizes by Anna Callais. Hats by Viv Knowland and the dramatic Gabriela Ligenza.

Regular customers (and new ones) are well looked after by the knowledgeable six-strong Image team. They produce a regular fashion newsletter giving a brief outline of their collections. IMAGE ITALIA in Shires Yard forms the Italian connection (see below).

....

IMAGE ITALIA
9 Shires Yard
Milsom Street
Bath
0225 447359

Open: 9.30 to 5.30 Mon. to Sat.
Credit Cards: Access, American Express, Diners Club, Visa

The Italian outpost of IMAGE in Northumberland Place. Devoted to the MaxMara range – MaxMara, Sportmax, Penny Black, I Blues, Marella, Weekend. Sit and watch a video of the latest collections.

....

SQUARE
3–4 The Corridor
Bath
0225 464997

Open: 10.00 to 6.00 Mon. to Sat.
Credit Cards: Access, American Express, Diners Club, Visa

Shop for cred designer casuals: Katherine Hamnett jeans and Hamnett II, Junior Gaultier, Soap Studio etc. in designer sizes 8 to 14.

....

MADELEINE ANN
11 Shires Yard
Bath
0225 448610

Open: 9.30 to 5.30 Mon. to Sat.
Credit Cards: Access, Visa

Elegant clothes in the affordable to
expensive range. Labels include
Ferre, Crisca, Odoi, sizes 8 to 16.
Three private changing rooms and
helpful informed staff. Belongs to
the MADELEINE ANN Midland
chain; there are branches in
SOLIHULL, STRATFORD ON AVON
and WORCESTER.

....

VIVIENNE SMITH
SIMPLY CLOTHES
15 New Bond Street
Bath
0225 310445

Open: 9.00 to 5.30 Mon. to Sat.
Credit Cards: Access, American
Express, Diners Club, Visa

Own label cotton dresses, soft
suits, long and short taffeta party
frocks all at sensible prices. For
more details see page 29. There are
also branches at BRISTOL,
GUILDFORD, HULL, LEEDS,
NOTTINGHAM, SHEFFIELD,
WAKEFIELD and YORK.

....

JANET WOOD FASHIONS
4a Queen Street
Bath
0225 446781

Open: 10.00 to 5.30 Mon. to Fri;
9.00 to 5.30 Sat.
Credit Cards: Access, American
Express, Diners Club, Visa

Friendly, unpressurized shopping
in a tiny shop made cosy with
settees and drapes. Lots of evening
wear (Candici); daywear from
Portara and Basler and a small
exclusive range from designer
Elaine Miller who specializes in
interesting mixed fabrics.
Exclusive range of ornate leather
belts from American designer
Carolyn Tanner. Sizes 8 to 16
(some larger sizes evening wear).
Prices range from £100.00 to
£300.00. Very helpful, informed
staff who actively encourage
browsing; coffee provided for
regulars. There is another Janet
Wood in YEOVIL.

....

Party Frocks

VERVE
18 Shires Yard
Milsom Street
Bath
0225 837392

Open: 9.30/10.00 to 5.30 Mon. to
Sat.
Credit Cards: Access, Diners Club,
Visa

Wonderful high beamed ceiling and
mahogany furniture give the shop a
comfortable feel. Evening gowns
and wedding dresses designed and

made up from a vast selection of scrumptious fabrics. They also sell some ready to wear clothes including some rather jazzy holiday stuff.

Hats

TITFERS
3 Shires Yard
Bath
0225 4486662

Open: 9.30 to 5.30 Mon. to Fri; 9.30 to 5.15 Sat.
Credit Cards: Access, American Express, Visa

Definitely the place for wedding hats: lots of veils and bright colours; also trendy trilbies and big floppy velvet caps.

Knitwear

AVOCA HANDWEAVERS
9 Cheap Street
Bath
0225 462165

Open: 9.30 to 5.30 Mon. to Sat; 10.30 to 5.00 SUNDAY.
Credit Cards: Access, American Express, Diners Club, Visa

Tiny outpost of the Irish company, featuring the same jewel coloured soft woollen shawls, capes, skirts and tops. See page 148.

BRISTOL

BOULES
68 Queens Road
Clifton
Bristol BS8 1NB
0272 24085

Open: 9.30 to 5.30 Mon. to Sat.
Credit Cards: Access, American Express, Diners Club, Visa

One of a small chain of shops selling reasonably priced smart and casual daywear for the under 35s. See CAMBRIDGE. Also in London (Covent Garden and Hammersmith) and EXETER.

SHIRES YARD
. . . .
The place to shop in Bath is Shires Yard, between Milsom Street and Broad Street.
Built in 1740 as stables, it is now transformed into a beautiful shopping arcade, housing some of the smartest shops in town.
. . . .
Most of them have bare blonde sandstone walls in keeping with the mellow surroundings.
. . . .

CHEQUERS
32 The Mall
Clifton Village
Bristol
0272 738653

Open: 9.00 to 5.30 Mon. to Sat.
Credit Cards: Access, American
Express, Diners Club, Visa

Small elegant shop in elegant
upmarket Clifton. Wearable mid-
to upper bracket clothes: Nicole
Farhi, Paul Costelloe, Unanyme,
MaxMara, Ginochietti, Blues Club,
Weekend; splendid collection of
Kay Cosserat smart separates that
are snapped up almost before they
are on the rails.
    Sizes 8-16/18 (they don't like to
be rigid as ranges differ); prices
affordable to expensive. Hats from
Rech and Costelloe to match their
clothes. Friendly, personal service.

HUDSON & HUDSON
37 Park Street
Bristol
0272 250730

Open: 9.30 to 5.30 Mon. to Fri; 9.30
to 6.00 Sat.
Credit Cards: Access, American
Express, Diners Club, Visa; own
Hudson & Hudson card

Cadet branch of the CARDIFF shop,
with much the same stock: fun
young labels (Ghost etc) and
affordable chic for both sexes.

VIVIENNE SMITH
SIMPLY CLOTHES
19 Union Street
Bristol
0272 298972

Open: 9.00 to 5.30 Mon. to Sat.
Credit Cards: Access, American
Express, Diners Club, Visa

Own label cotton dresses, soft
suits, long and short taffeta party
frocks all at sensible prices. For
more details see page 29. There are
also branches at BATH, GUILDFORD,
HULL, LEEDS, NOTTINGHAM,
SHEFFIELD, WAKEFIELD and YORK.

Hats

THAT HAT SHOP
52 Royal York Crescent
Clifton
Bristol
0272 738318

Open: 9.30 to 5.30 Mon. to Sat.
Credit Cards: Access, American
Express, Diners Club, Visa

Lovely Georgian shop; soft
lighting, pastel decor within. Hats
from Freddy Fox, Genevieve
Louis, Graham Smith, Peter
Bettley, Patricia; Kangol and
Merida in the cheaper line. The
place to go for special occasion hats:
at the top of the season they have up
to 4000 hats in stock – but if you still
can't find what you want, they can
have hats made up from your own
material. Jewellery from Christian
Dior, Nina Ricci, Attwood.

CORNWALL

FALMOUTH

BELINDA RUSHWORTH-LUND
September Cottage
Helford Village
nr Falmouth
Cornwall
0326 23667

Wonderful collection of delicious knitwear for children and grown ups. Choose from the existing design collection and name your size and colour (expect to pay between £50.00 and £100.00 for an adult jumper); or commission an individual one-off (price negotiable). All natural fibres. Belinda Rushworth-Lund is the author of *Knit a Nursery Rhyme* (Bloomsbury 1989).

DEVON

DAWLISH

SARAH VIVIAN GALLERY
2 Queen Street
Dawlish EX7 9HB

Open: 10.00 to 6.00 Mon. to Sat.
Credit Cards: Access, American Express, Diners Club, Visa

A compact treasure chest of handcrafted clothes up in the heart of Dawlish, off the tourist track. It really is a gallery: Sarah Vivian is

herself a weaver, and over 140 other individual craftspeople are represented here: clothes of all kinds, hand painted silk scarves, marbled silk separates, padded patchwork jackets, hand made boots and shoes, accessories: everything is a one-off. If you like what you see, you can commission one just like it in your size, change the colour, even modify the design. For logistic reasons, most suppliers are from the south, but there is one knitter in Orkney who has to row her wares over to the mainland before they even get to the post office – what could be more romantic? There are monthly exhibitions, showing works by groups of allied craftspeople, or demonstrating techniques. A workshop at the back takes care of made to measure commissions. Wonderful place for people with an eye for individual, exclusive clothes.

EXETER

BOULES
75 Queen Street
Exeter EX4 3RX
0392 214154

Open: 9.30 to 5.30 Mon. to Sat.
Credit Cards: Access, American Express, Diners Club, Visa

One of a small chain of shops selling reasonably priced smart and casual daywear for the under 35s. See CAMBRIDGE. Also in London (Covent Garden and Hammersmith) and BRISTOL.

DUKES
Harlequins
Paul Street
Exeter EX4 3TT
0392 74840

Open: 9.00 to 5.30 Mon. to Sat.
Credit Cards: Access, Visa; Hoopers
Account Card

The newest and possibly spankiest
of the ever expanding Hoopers, the
family firm which is rapidly
colonising the wealthy towns of
England. DUKES is the fashion-
dedicated store, a spacious, airy
marble floored emporium, with
comfy settees to sit on while you
contemplate your purchases.
Labels include Jean Muir,
Valentino, Escada, I Blues, Fink,
Marina Rinaldi, La Squadra, Betty
Barclay, Diane Freis, Hidy
Misawa; accessories from Gucci,
jewellery from Angie Gooderham,
Butler & Wilson; Mitzi Lorenz
hats. Alterations and adjustments
undertaken by resident tailor.
Regular fashion shows and
promotions, so it is worth getting
yourself on the mailing list.

There are other Hoopers in
CHELTENHAM, CHICHESTER,
COLCHESTER, TORQUAY,
TUNBRIDGE WELLS, WILMSLOW.

POSH
16 South Street
Exeter EX1 1DX
0392 52368

Open: 9.30 to 5.30 Mon. to Sat.
Credit Cards: Access, American
Express, Diners Club, Visa

Small, pretty shop with friendly

staff, sofas to sit on and coffee to
drink. Well chosen labels: Betty
Jackson, Nicole Farhi, Spanish
designer Roberto Verinno and
Outlander. Sizes 8 to 16, and free
alteration service.

WILLY'S
24 Gandy Street
Exeter EX4 3LS
0392 56010

Open: 9.30 to 5.30 Mon. to Sat.
Credit Cards: Access, American
Express, Diners Club, Visa

Totally wonderful shop in Gandy
Street (pedestrianised
cobblestones, lots of jolly shops
and pubs). Gorgeous neoclassical
interior, black and white terrazzo
floor, marbled walls, huge arched
windows and an enormous live
fountain in the middle. Vivaldi
tunes, naturally, plus excellent
modern music. The eponymous
Willy is a golden retriever, now
somewhat struck in years but still
getting into the office every day.

Top-hole labels (sizes 8 to 14):
Sara Sturgeon (main and diffusion),
Joe Casely-Hayford, Ghost,
Twisted Sister, Simple Standards,
Ici la Fille, Soap Studio, Le Garage,
Moschino, Rocco Barocco, Junior
Gaultier, Quaker (well cut British
stuff in the Ally Capellino mode);
hats from Sandra Phillips and
Bernstock and Spiers: shoes from
Emma Hope, Pellini, Willi van
Roy. AND prices are up to 25%
less than London...
unsurprisingly, many Londoners
think it's well worth a trip.

PLYMOUTH

CIRCUS

8 Drake Circus
Plymouth
0752 221804

Open: 10.00 to 5.30 Mon. to Sat.
Credit Cards: Access, Visa

Small shop selling clothes for men
and women (Ally Capellino suits
for the chaps). Small and select
number of labels: Sara Sturgeon,
Moschino, Neoline and Ghost.
Sizes 8 to 14. Excellent extremely
stylish own label (Circus)
collection which changes each
season: last summer it was 20s
cruisewear inspired; for the winter
it was loads of velvet; this
summer's collection eagerly
awaited.

....

SISTER CODY

15 Old Town Street
Plymouth
0752 600947

Open: 9.30 to 6.00 Mon. to Sat.
Credit Cards: Access, American
Express, Visa

Sister shop (of course) to Cody (for
men) next door. Smart designer
casual: Valentino jeans collection,
Armani ditto, Best Company,
Katherine Hamnett and Hamnett
II, Mulberry accessories.
   They used to stock Ralph Lauren
and other grown up frocks, but
Plymouth was not quite ready for
it...jolly, friendly shop.

....

TOP SECRET BOUTIQUE
2 Market Avenue
Plymouth PL1 1PQ
0752 662209

Open: 9.30 to 5.00 Mon. to Sat.
Credit Cards: Access, American
Express, Diners Club, Visa

Very strong on special occasion
wear; very good personal service –
they will tactfully save you from
the social death of wearing the same
dress as your neighbour to the local
hunt ball. Labels include Verf,
Puccini, Candici. Matching hats
available.

....

TORQUAY

HOOPERS
The Strand
Torquay
0803 212754

Open: 9.15 to 5.30 Mon. to Sat.
Credit Cards: Access, American
Express, Diners Club, Visa;
Hoopers Account Card

One of the Hoopers fashion
oriented department stores: clothes
from Escada, Mondi, Marella,
Betty Barclay, OuiSet, Gibi;
Marina Rinaldi and Patrizia for the
16+.
   There are Hoopers in
CHELTENHAM, CHICHESTER,
COLCHESTER, TUNBRIDGE WELLS,
WILMSLOW. See also Dukes of
EXETER.

....

TAVISTOCK

STATUS
11 West Street
Tavistock
0822 615107

Open: 9.30 to 5.30 Mon. to Sat.
Credit Cards: Access, Visa

Megachic shop rapidly becoming the in place to meet in Tavistock. Distinct Athenian theme: columns, glass, statues and wonderful changing room curtains patterned with Greek gods; very friendly atmosphere and staff; lots of lovely clothes in the mid price range: Java, Naughty and Next the main labels: sizes 8 to 14; voile prints, strong colours, lined linen suits. Party frocks are a new venture, starting this spring. This is an extremely popular shop in the West Country: people bus in from Plymouth to visit it. Regular customers become members of the Status club (about 300 so far): there are special members-only sales nights, fashion shows and previews. Sales for everybody twice a year slash 10% to 50% from prices.

DORSET

WIMBORNE

COUNTRY CLASSICS
King's Court
Wimborne
0202 881477

Open: 9.30 to 5.30 Mon. to Fri; 9.30 to 5.00 Sat.
Credit Cards: Access, Visa

Sloane heaven in the country; the place to buy everything Barbour in Dorset. Also sell classic knitwear (Lyle & Scott) and good solid British clothes (Aquascutum). Great place to spot the country gentlemen in his natural habitat. The shop is small but very well organised and the staff friendly and helpful. People come from far flung places for the reassurance of shopping here.

GLOUCESTERSHIRE

CHELTENHAM

JUDY GRAHAM
21 The Promenade
Cheltenham
0242 517726

Open: 9.30 to 5.30 Mon. to Sat.
Credit Cards: Access, American Express, Diners Club, Visa

Second branch of the Judy Graham in CIRENCESTER, selling the same upmarket classy classic labels: Paul Costelloe, Edina Ronay, Mulberry.

ALISON HARRISON
3 The Courtyard
Montpellier
Cheltenham
0242 519452

Open: 9.30 to 5.30 Mon. to Sat.
Credit Cards: Access,
American Express, Diners
Club, Visa

One of the small chain of
terminally chic Annabel/
Alison Harrison shops full of
mouthwatering designer
labels (Mani, Lauren etc). See
BATH. Also at OXFORD and
LEAMINGTON SPA.

....

HOOPERS LIMITED
The Promenade
Cheltenham G50 1LE
0242 527505

Open: 9.15 to 5.30 Mon. to Sat.
Credit Cards: Access, American
Express, Diners Club, Visa;
Hoopers Account Card

One of the Hoopers fashion
oriented department stores. Wide
range of mid price and upper
bracket euro labels and a 16 plus
department; alteration service
available.
   There are Hoopers in
CHICHESTER, COLCHESTER,
TORQUAY, TUNBRIDGE WELLS,
WILMSLOW. See also Dukes of
EXETER.

....

TIZZIE D
11 Montpellier Arcade
Cheltenham
0242 584188

Open: 9.30 to 5.30 Mon. to Sat.
Credit Cards: Access, Visa

Small but grand looking shop, all
brass fittings and chandeliers.
Strong range of German label
evening wear, sizes 8 to 18. Grown
up dressing.

....

TRAPEZE
50 Regent Street
Cheltenham
0242 577937

Open: 10.00 to 6.00 Mon. to Fri;
9.30 to 6.00 Sat.
Credit Cards: Access, American
Express, Mastercard, Visa

Light, bright shop for snappy
dressers: Ghost, Twisted Sister,
Junior Gaultier, original Wallabees.

....

Jewellery

BEARDS
70 The Promenade
Cheltenham
0242 516238

Open: 9.15 to 5.15 Mon. to Sat.
Credit Cards: Access, American
Express, Visa

Wonderfully luxurious jewellers
stocking serious rocks and gold,
Mikimoto cultured pearls and
inexpensive(ish) gemstone
jewellery. Also the big time
watches: Rotary, Cartier,
Longines.

....

Dress Hire

SOIREE
9 Rotunda Terrace
Cheltenham
0242 522136

Open: 9.30 to 5.00 Mon. to Sat.
Credit Cards: Access, Visa

Very glamorous party clothes for hire at a remarkable £45.00 a time. Beaded numbers by Serenade. Not for the portly: sizes 10, 12 and 14 only.

Made to Measure

THE WENDY HOUSE
14 St James Street
Cheltenham
0242 513087

Open: 9.30 to 5.30 Mon. to Fri; 9.30 to 4.30 Sat; or by appointment
Credit Cards: American Express, Visa

A gem. Evening dresses and ball gowns handmade in beautiful fabrics by Wendy and Sophie Jackson in their workroom above the shop. The ready to wear range (sizes 8 to 16) can be altered to suit individual bodily quirks, or you can have a one-off custom made (larger sizes possible – up to 24). Allow two weeks to a month, depending on the degree of elaboration. A photo album of satisfied customers wearing previous confections helps the undecided to choose designs. The changing/fitting room is spacious and the Jacksons take infinite time and trouble to make sure everything is just right. Prices are very agreeable: from £55.00 for a short number; £300.00 to £400.00 for a no-holds-barred ballgown.

Shoes

PRAGNELL SHOES
2 The Courtyard
Montpellier
Cheltenham
0242 577908

Open: 9.30 to 5.30 Mon. to Sat.
Credit Cards: Access, American Express, Diners Club, Visa

Wonderful Robert Clergerie and Stephane Kelian shoes: what else is there? Possibly the only shop you can buy Kelian outside London (and Barnsley). Prices start around £90.00 but who cares. Sizes 3 to 8. Handbags to match made especially by Baldanini at the persuasion of Mr George Pragnell himself. Pay between £100.00 and £200.00 but you won't find one elsewhere. Also decorative parapluies from France, unusual jewellery from America (clean, modern designs in costume gold and silver); delicious hand made gloves from Paris (around £90.00) and very nice little suede and leather gloves in all colours for about a third of the price.

CIRENCESTER

JUDY GRAHAM
Northway House
Cirencester
02855 659119

Open: 9.30 to 5.30 Mon. to Sat.
Credit Cards: Access, American
Express, Diners Club, Visa

Smart comfortable shop for the
well heeled fashion conscious
county set; stylish classics from
Paul Costelloe, impeccable
Mulberry accessories, Edina Ronay
knitwear. Sizes 8 to 18. Also in
CHELTENHAM.

....

SOMERSET

YEOVIL

JANET WOOD FASHIONS
13 Wine Street
Yeovil
0935 29915

Open: 10.00 to 5.00 Mon. to Fri;
9.00 to 5.30 Sat.
Credit Cards: Access, Diners Club,
Visa

Larger than the Bath shop, but the
same unhurried and friendly
atmosphere created by settees and
drapes. Slightly less formal
separates – jolly shorts, shirts,
cropped pants; lots of special
occasion wear; ballgowns to buy
and hire (sizes 8 to 20, average price
£150.00; hire for £45.00). Zillions

of hats, some of which can also be
hired. Clever accessories and much
fun costume jewellery. Relaxed
shopping for all ages at very good
prices. See also Janet Wood
Fashions BATH.

....

WILTSHIRE

MARLBOROUGH

SPANGLES
High Street
Marlborough
0672 516353

Open: 9.30 to 5.30 Mon. to Sat.
Credit Cards: Access, American
Express, Visa

Jolly friendly staff in a neatly
organised shop which dresses the
jeunesse dorée of Marlborough.
Casual separates and loads of jeans
collections. Good value prices and,
surprisingly for a young persons'
shop, v. nice private changing
rooms.

....

SALISBURY

Hats

THAT HAT SHOP
19 Brown Street
Salisbury
0722 332888

Open: 9.30 to 5.00 Mon. to Sat.
Credit Cards: Access, American
Express, Diners Club, Visa

NOT connected to the concern of
the same name in BRISTOL. Tiny
shop celebrating its 10th
anniversary, crammed with hats at
all prices: modest straws from
under a tenner to Philip Somerville
objets d'art at £200.00 or so. Peter
Bettley, Marida (the hat monger to
the larger headed) Kangol,
Bermona. Specialities are jolly
unstructured tweed and cord
floppy hats by Hat Attack (about
£15.00 up) and unusual rococo soft
velvet numbers beset with beads
and buttons by Jean Chisholm
(about £40.00). Special occasion
hats of course; you can also have a
hat made to measure: price
depends on which milliner label
you choose.

Shoes

RAFFINEE
39 High Street
Salisbury
0722 33475

Open: 9.30 to 5.30 Mon. to Sat.
Credit Cards: Access, American
Express, Visa

Wonderful Trollopian setting
opposite the cathedral close for
small indy shoe shop, owned and
run by Trudy Harris. Judicious
buying from 18 different suppliers
look reminiscent of Fratelli Rossetti
but with bags of choice: Valmy
Moda, Balnar, Elena de Marco,
Alberto Gozzi, Lorbac, Linea
Bruna; v. stylish toe-thong sandals
from Rapisardi for the summer.
Very generous size range – 33 to
43½. Good range of creamy white
shoes and pumps for weddings, all
of which can be dyed after the event
to match party wear. Lots of lovely
bags from Italy and Finland;
jewellery from Flash Harry; scarves
from Balenciaga and local heroine
Georgina von Etzdorf (her factory
is close to the city).

Special Sizes

CLASSIC PLUS
75 New Street
Salisbury
0722 290936

Open: 9.30 to 5.30 Mon. to Sat.
Credit Cards: Access, American
Express, Diners Club, Visa

Excellent range of daywear for the
generously proportioned: elegant
labels: Patrizia, Marina Rinaldi. No
shoes or hats. A sister shop, Classic
Corner at 12, The Maltings
(Salisbury's new riverside
shopping precinct) sells dateless
clothes – Rodier, Marion
Donaldson, Aquascutum, Dax – in
sizes 10 to 20.

EAST ANGLIA

··········

CAMBRIDGESHIRE, ESSEX, NORFOLK, SUFFOLK

After some decades in the fashion doldrums, East Anglia is galloping up on the style rails, fuelled by the expanding commuter belt and the growing disinclination of Londoners to shop in London. Go to Cambridge for well presented fashion in sublime surroundings; Chelmsford for grown-up dressing; Newmarket for racy chic; Norwich for classics with a twist.

CAMBRIDGESHIRE

CAMBRIDGE

BOULES
5 Rose Crescent
Cambridge
CB2 3LL
0223 321156

Open: 9.30 to 5.30 Mon. to Sat.
Credit Cards: Access, Visa

By all accounts this small, friendly, crammed shop is much better than the Covent Garden branch. All own label stuff: smart or casual daywear for the under 35s size 8 to 14 (there is a communal dressing room). Reasonable prices. Accessories particularly moreish. They have v. good sales involving major reductions – three or four a year, at the usual times and when stock dictates.

Also in EXETER, London (Covent Garden and Hammersmith) and BRISTOL.

CAMBRIDGE MARKET
· · · ·
Cambridge market is open six days a week and has a variety of good speciality clothes stalls.

Look out for home knits, recherche hats, jewellery and ethnic togs.
· · · ·

FLAPPERS
84 Mill Road
Cambridge CB1 2AL
0223 68442

Open: 10.00 to 6.00 Mon. to Sat.
Credit Cards: Visa

V. nice shop selling period clothes from Victorian to 60s, with emphasis on the extravaganzas of the 1920s (hence the name). Expect to pay anything from £3.00 to £200.00. Very popular with students from the nearby tech. You can also hire a Flapper Outfit or a new ballgown for the May Ball (between £20.00 and £40.00 for a weekend).

If you flag, there is a coffee shop upstairs (different owner) very 50s with relaxing jazz.

JANE
17–19 Sussex Street
Cambridge
0223 314455

Open: 9.00 to 5.30 Mon. to Sat.
Credit Cards: Access, American Express, Diners Club, Visa

Three hand-carved oak horses, retired from fairground roundabouts, lure people into this lovely old shop. Pink like the other JANEs, but with different, more reposeful atmosphere to suit the meditative charms of Cambridge. Good size range (8 to 20): Laurel, Mondi, Yarell for daywear, but they major in special occasion dressing with magnifico ballgowns from Diane Freis, Coterie, Carole Lee...and Caroline Charles.

Customers come from far afield, many from London, for the excellent personal service. And American tourists try to buy the horses almost every day...

Also at NEWMARKET and NORWICH

....

PRIMAVERA
51 Trumpington Street
Cambridge
0223 460228

Open: 9.30 to 5.30 Mon. to Fri; 9.00 to 5.30 Sat.
Credit Cards: Access, American Express, Visa

and
16 King's Parade
Cambridge
0223 357708

Open: 9.30 to 5.30 Mon. to Fri; 9.00 to 5.30 Sat.
Credit Cards: Access, American Express, Visa

Fresh, light uncluttered shop, lovely stylish clothes; Betty Jackson range, and for the summer cotton jersey separates from Tehen (the French label stocked in The Vestry, South Molton Street); Viv Knowland hats and Georgina von Etzdorf scarves. Clothes are not ghettoed into 'collections' but put together in an interesting way – live wardrobe planning in fact. Sizes 8 to 14/16. They also have lovely big bright clothes for sizes 18 to 26 from Finnish designers Marimekko and Vuoko.

PRIMAVERA in King's Parade (about 10 minutes walk away) is the revamped Craft Shop they started off with. It's bigger, but in the same style; this season they are stocking Katharine Hamnett jeans and the Hamnett II diffusion line.

Staff are helpful, informed and enthusiastic; customers come here to get away from the often brutalizing experience of shopping in London.

....

PETERBOROUGH

VALENTINA
2 Park Road
Peterborough PE1 2TD
0733 558896

Open: 9.00 to 5.30 Mon. to Sat.
Credit Cards: Access, American Express, Diners Club, Visa

One of the trio of smart green and white shops majoring in Italian and French clothes (Mani and the like). Sizes 8 to 20. See Valentina in LEICESTER. There is also a branch in NOTTINGHAM.

....

ESSEX

CHELMSFORD

GEORGINA DE RITTER
12 Baddow Road
Chelmsford CM6 3EZ
0245 258808

Open: 9.30 to 5.00 Mon. to Fri;
closes 1.00 on Wed; 9.30 to 5.30
Sat.
Credit Cards: Access, Visa

Distinctive black and white old-
style building houses a shop that
majors in what to wear for special
occasions (although they also stock
smart casual wear). Amazingly
helpful patient staff who will advise
those boggling at the thought of
dressing up. Very strong on
wardrobe planning: regular
customers who move out of the
area come back to stock up. Sizes
are 8 to 16 and they have a 'treasure'
who can do magical alterations.
Labels include Coterie, Parigi,
Puccini, Synonyme, Hesselhoj,
Frank Usher; hats from Peter
Bettley and Coterie; bags, shoes
and jewellery.

WRAPS
19 Baddow Road
Chelmsford
0245 265527

Open: 9.30 to 5.00 Mon. to Fri;
closes 1.00 on Wed; 9.45 to 5.30
Sat.
Credit Cards: Access, American
Express, Visa

Small shop in old typically Essex
building; stock is gradually being
revised by new owner. Strong
Italian presence, Vera di Pozzo
knitwear (expect to pay £200 to
£300), silk skirts, lovely bags and
belts; also I Blues, Blues Company.
Sizes range from 8 to 16. A small
range of French lingerie – Miss
Lou, and soon Huit.

COLCHESTER

AMBIANCE
87 Crouch Street
Colchester CO3 3E2
0206 570433

Open: 9.30 to 5.30 Mon. to Fri; 9.30
to 5.00 Sat.
Credit Cards: Access, American
Express, Diners Club, Visa

Small shop with welcoming
atmosphere and five helpful staff.
Stylish daywear and smart casuals
for professional thirtysomethings.
Good labels: Karl Lagerfeld KL,
Laurel, Bleu Blanc Rouge,
Amuleti, Janina Schreck, Gail
Hoppen; sizes 10 to 18, and
alteration service provided.

HOOPERS OF COLCHESTER
LIMITED
Queen Street
Colchester CO1 2PN
0206 41311

Open: 9.15 to 5.30 Mon. to Sat.
Credit Cards: Access, American
Express, Diners Club, Visa;
Hoopers Account card

Another of Hooper's transformations; this compact department store backs onto the huge but not unpleasant shopping precinct that dominates central Colchester. Most designer labels are sold, and they have their own Hoopers label. Sizes range from 8 to 24; staff are informed and helpful and clothes are well displayed in collections. Alteration service.

There are other Hoopers in CHELTENHAM, CHICHESTER, TORQUAY, TUNBRIDGE WELLS, WILMSLOW. See also Dukes of EXETER.

MONK'S DORMITORY
31 Sir Isaac's Walk
Colchester
0206 577188

Open: 9.30 to 5.30 Mon. to Sat.
Credit cards: Access, Visa

Intriguing shop, strong on the stable theme: all pine, saddlery and grain bins. Yummy thoroughbred labels: Caroline Charles, Ally Capellino, Arabella Pollen, Terence Nolder, Susan Croft silks; lower price bracket includes Joyce Riding's Qui range of easy to wear linen and cotton casuals. Sizes 8 to 16. Lovely belts (hanging on the saddles) and jewellery (displayed in a glassed over butcher's block). Rosy lingerie and a delicious new range of silk and pure cotton for next season. Wedding wear upstairs. The owner has a genuine 11th century monastery in nearby and frighteningly ancient Coggeshall: hence the name.

ROCHELLE
10 Headgate Buildings
Sir Isaac's Walk
Colchester
0206 570811

Open: 9.00 to 5.30 (or longer if you want) Mon. to Sat.
Credit Cards: Access, Visa

Tiny shop dedicated to the Escada range, mostly daywear and separates (sizes 10 to 16); Langani jewellery; very friendly obliging staff who will tailor the shop hours to their customers' needs.

ELD LANE
....

Tiny, ancient Eld Lane has toughed it out through interminable building developments, finally emerging as the Newburgh Street of East Anglia: lots of laid back style and a poseur's paradise on Saturdays. *Caboodle* (no. 41) sells men's and women's Spanish leather shoes, also Seducta, Mr Seymour and all-leather Nickels runabouts. Sister shop (no. 13) *Syboe* (Scottish for Spring Onion!) for young casual fashion – InWear, Fenn, Wright & Manson, Sun and Sand; *Arana* at no. 5 is for relaxed grown-up dressing: Joseph, Mulberry, MaxMara, Taverniti and Naf Naf.

....

NORFOLK

NORWICH

BOWLERS
8 Bedford Street
Norwich
0603 619085

Open: 9.30 to 6.00 Mon. to Sat.
Credit Cards: Access, Visa

Relaxed, unsnooty shop in *the* street for small independents in Norwich. There are two floors, menswear below and the girls on top. Very wearable clothes and classics with a bit of a kick for the 25+: Laurel, Crisca, Nicole Farhi, Amuleti, A Priori, Jousse, Benny Ong, Terence Nolder; Sandra Phillips hats. Sizes 8 to 16, and an alteration service.

JANE
7 St Stephen's Plain
Norwich
Norfolk
0603 764400

Open: 9.00 to 5.30 Mon. to Sat.
Credit Cards: Access, American Express, Diners Club, Visa

This is a new JANE, opened in January; here the Jane pink is teamed with turquoise and there are exotic tented ceilings; it is slightly smaller than the Newmarket store, and very friendly; all the right labels – Mondi, Escada, Betty Barclay, Louis Feraud, and lots of short and long cocktail and evening dresses (sizes 8 to 20). Thompson Beanland

hats and lashings of lovely jewellery.

Also in CAMBRIDGE and NEWMARKET

NORWICH

LOLIPOP
3 Westlegate
Norwich
0603 630474

Open: 10.00 to 5.30 Mon. to Sat.
Credit Cards: Access, American Express, Visa

Casual wear for the young: InWear, French Connection, BikBok, Mexx in sizes 8 to 16. Ultramodern shop, very jolly atmosphere... and yes it is Lolipop with one 'l'.

SUFFOLK

IPSWICH

CLOUDS
24 Tackett Street
Ipswich
0473 215309

Open: 9.30 to 5.00 Tues. to Sat.
Credit Cards: Access, American Express, Diners Club, Visa; own Wardrobe account

Two floors of smart labels covering the 8 to 14 size range. Nicole Farhi, L'Estelle, Gaston Jaunet, Paul Costelloe's Dressage line; Bally shoes and Della hats. Alteration service and coffee.

NEWMARKET

JANE
29 High Street
Newmarket
0638 668031

Open: 9.00 to 5.30 Mon. to Fri; 9.00
to 5.00 Sat.
Credit Cards: Access, American
Express, Diners Club, Visa

Easy parking

There are three JANEs, all themed in
pink on pink: Newmarket is the
flagship, with appropriate gold
trimmings. A favourite with the
racing set, it glitters with smart
daywear and special occasion
dressing. Upstairs find Laurel,
Strasser, Basler, Mondi; Escada,
Frank Usher and Bernshaw
evening wear. Downstairs features
casual separates and coordinates
(Betty Barclay, Olsen, Bianca).
Also La Perla, Gossard and Lejaby
lingerie, Louis Feraud robes and
wraps, hats belts and jewellery.

Although sizes range from 8 to
20, they always have a good range
of 8s, of which they sell squillions –
presumably to jockeys' partners (or
lady jockeys).

Also downstairs is a WINE BAR!
Noted in the E. Ronay *Just a Bite*
guide, it features soup, homemade
bread and scrummy cakes – so
much for size 8.

There are also JANES at
CAMBRIDGE and NORWICH.

WOODBRIDGE

ADAM'S APPLE
1 The Thoroughfare
Woodbridge IP2 1AA
03943 4685

Open: 9.00 to 5.30 Mon. to Sat.
Credit Cards: Access, American
Express, Diners Club, Visa

Good range of day and casual wear
from Gardeur, Ports International,
Ideas Plus, Susan Crofts for the
25+. Sizes 10 to 18 and alterations
can be arranged. Helpful staff and
personal service; regular clientele
receive a questionnaire and a
newsletter is in the offing.
Shrubland Hall Health Centre is
nearby, and keen healthies can buy
their Rassurelle swimwear here:
they keep a very good range in
stock all year.

SUSAN ROOKE
1 Market Hill
Woodbridge
03943 36570

Open: 9.30 to 5.15 Mon. to Fri;
closes 1.00 Weds; 9.30 to 5.00 Sat.
Credit Cards: Access, Visa

Scrumptious shop, recently hugely
expanded: almost too much to
choose from; shoes from over 60
designers (lots of Italians); clothes
in 8 to 16/18 from (among others)
Dressage, Jean Muir Studio, B.
Oldfield 1992; Jean Claude,
Synonyme; knitwear from Hyne &
Eames, Joye & Fun; jewellery from
Folli Follie, Angie Gooderham; silk
jewellery from Sara Marr.

THE HOME COUNTIES

· · · · · · · · · ·

**BERKSHIRE,
BUCKINGHAMSHIRE, GREATER
LONDON (the late lamented
Middlesex), HERTFORDSHIRE,
KENT (the part nearest London),
SURREY**

Increasingly, the home counties present
a very attractive alternative to
metropolitan shopping. Visit Amersham
and find an unexpected designer haven;
Beaconsfield for ultra chic; Maidenhead
for style and customer care; Weybridge
(especially Waterloo Terrace) for
luxurious shoes and accessories.

BERKSHIRE

REBECCA
26 Queen Street
Maidenhead
0628 36912

Open: 9.00 to 5.30/6.00 Mon. to Sat.
Credit Cards: Access, American Express, Diners Club, Visa; own Wardrobe six month interest free account

Stylish high-ceilinged shop (it used to be an old fashioned butcher's emporium) selling designer labels especially selected to blend and mix with each other: Ginochietti, MaxMara, Weekend, Blues, Club, Marella, Arabella Pollen, Edina Ronay, Paul Costelloe, Trussardi; Gail Hoppen snazzy cocktail suits; great range of mock exotic leather belts and bags from Italy (only available here and at Harvey Nichols) looking just like the real thing but soothing your conscience as well as your bank balance (they sell at v. reasonable £25.00 to £40.00). Chantal gilty jewellery. It's a pleasure to shop here – lots of blonde wood and fresh flowers, and very friendly helpful staff. Regular customers are loved to death: invitation champagne brunches for new season launches, special previews, and a mailing list in which they are classified by size and taste so they can be the first to know about new lines. Rebecca II is in the pipeline.

BUCKINGHAMSHIRE

AMERSHAM

PAUL COSTELLOE
25 High Street
Amersham HP7 07P
0494 724717

Open: 10.00 to 5.30 Mon. to Sat.
Credit Cards: Access, Diners Club, Visa

Charming small Georgian shop (rustic beams inside) is a fitting showcase for Irish designer Paul Costelloe's classic wearable clothes. This is the only exclusively Paul Costelloe outlet in the country. Both collections carried: Dressage, the diffusion line, starts at £75.00; the main collection at £100.00. Sizes are 8 to 16, and there is an alteration service. Private dressing rooms, coffee, and friendly relaxed, laid-back staff who don't need to hustle because 'the clothes sell themselves'. Sales in second week of January and July. Although there is no fully fledged mail order system, they will post items to regular customers.

AMBERS OF AMERSHAM
The Mill Stream
London Road
Old Amersham HP7 9OA
0494 722471

Open: 9.00 to 5.30 Mon. to Sat.
Credit Cards: Access, American
Express, Diners Club, Visa

Excellent parking front and rear

Not so much a shop as a store,
Ambers is owned and run by ex
Hartnell model Carla Cameron and
her son Alistair. A charming
historic building with exposed
beams featuring the soothing
tinkling of a real millstream
running through the middle (lunch
or take coffee on its banks).
Unsurprisingly, the theme of the
shop is amber (bags, decor). Very
personal service to large, loyal
clientele and attracts many
shoppers who are tired of London.
Much posting to regular
customers. Labels include Escada,
YSL, Louis Feraud, Xandra
Rhodes, Nicole Farhi, Terence
Nolder, Benny Ong, Roland
Klein, Caroline Charles; also own
label smart daywear (Alistair at
Ambers); lingerie and swimwear
from La Perla; hats from Philip
Somerville, Peter Bettley, Freddy
Fox, Graham Smith and own
milliner Eda Rose; shoes from
Gina, Scada. Shoe and bag dyeing
and made to order hats. Ambers is
very strong on larger sizes (goes
from 8 to 24) but does not believe in
ghettoing them into a separate
department. Strong Marina Rinaldi
range. There is an alteration service
(own workroom) and Alistair

Cameron will make one-offs for
regular customers.

BEACONSFIELD

CLICHE
Burkes Court
Station Road
Beaconsfield

and 12 Station Road
Beaconsfield
0494 6768887

Open: 9.30 to 5.30 Mon. to Sat.
Credit Cards: Access, American
Express, Visa

Two branches of the same shop on
opposite sides of the road. The
Burkes Court shop is large,
spacious and sophisticated in the
minimal chic style and sells
MaxMara, Maska and Mani to
hardworking, elegant career
women. They wear the clothes, the
clothes don't wear them. The
Station Road shop is for ladies who
lunch: (Ginochietti, Byblos,
Chacok) and is more intimate; four
small rooms, coffee, altogether
more leisurely. Both shops carry
Pellini and designer jewellery; also
Fratelli Rossetti shoes (one of the
few out of town stockists).
Moschino is anticipated for the next
season. Sizes are 8 to 16, but they
are especially good on the smaller
sizes.

MARLOW

RIVE GAUCHE
71 High Street
Marlow SL7 1AB
06284 74472

Open: 9.30 to 5.30 Mon. to Sat.
Credit Cards: Access, American
Express, Diners Club, Visa

A slice of Bond Street in Bucks;
ultra-elegant shop strong on French
and German style: Feraud and
Feraud Set, all the Mondi range,
Krisca, Gaston Jaunet and Karl
Lagerfeld KL. Special occasion
wear from Diane Freis. Sizes 10 to
16, and prices to match the labels.

Lingerie

ENCHANTE
6 Burkes Parade
Beaconsfield
0494 678148

Open: 9.30 to 5.30 Mon. to Sat.
Credit Cards: Access, American
Express, Diners Club, Visa

Comprehensive La Perla
collection, bras, briefs, slips,
swimwear, robes and scent. Bra
sizes 32a to 40dd, Nightwear (La
Perla, Jane Woolrich) sizes 10 to 16.
Interesting selection of tights
including the French Osé sheer
lycra; towelling robes from La
Perla, Egeria; leisurewear (après
ski, post sun-bed) from Jean Le
Duc, Ken Done, Möve. Very
strong on swimwear – Liza Bruce,
Gottex, jolly Ken Done, Armonia,
Aquasuit (sizes 8 to 18, up to dd cup

sizes). Regular swimwear days for
bright customers in the know –
glass of champagne and a free
fashion show. Large(ish) shop, as
lingerie shops go, a little bit out of
the ordinary. Friendly, helpful
staff: gift wrapping and delivery.

HERTFORDSHIRE

Party Frocks

JUST FOR THE NIGHT
80 Sandridge Road
St Albans
0727 40759

Open: 9.00 to 4.00 Mon. to Fri; late
(7.00) Thurs; 10.00 to 4.00 Sat; also
by appointment
Credit Cards: Access, American
Express, Diners Club, Visa

Stun your friends and alarm your
enemies by hiring a sumptuous ball
gown or evening gown for the
night, plus all the trimmings (not
shoes). Short and long from simple
to OTT dresses from Bernshaw,
John Charles, Wim Hemminck etc
in sizes 8 to 20. Choice of jewellery
in various styles. Prices from
£40.25 to £57.50 depending on the
dress, and a deposit of £80.00 (a
cheque will do) gives you a
weekend's worth of glam. They
plan to have special occasion suits
and posh suits later in the year; hats
from about £10.00, suits as yet
unpriced. Excellent notion for
thrifty partygoers. There are more
Just for the Nights: see page 157.

STRIDES
6 George Street
St Albans
0727 31154

and 12 Holywell Hill
St Albans
0727 62747

Open: 9.00 to 5.30 Mon. to Sat.
Credit Cards: Access, American
Express, Diners Club, Visa

Tiny shop crammed with all the
right stuff – no room for minor
details such as decor; upmarket
labels in a friendly, unpretentious
atmosphere: Mondi, Portara,
Emmanuelle Khanh, Trixie
Schober, Guy Laroche, Beged
D'Or. Sizes 10 to 14/16. Just
around the corner is the Holywell
Hill branch, presenting a younger
zappier style: Betty Jackson,
Marella, OuiSet; and swimwear,
accessories and T-shirts from
dazzling Oz, Ken Done. Very
matey staff.

Made to Measure

DEBORAH AUGIER
4 Guildford Road
St Albans
0727 37655

Hand built special occasion wear
for the individualist (beading a
speciality). Especially good at the
extremes of the size spectrum
(tinies and giants). Deborah Augier
(ex London School of Fashion,
Donald Campbell) has been
established for eight years. She will
discuss your desires with you,

make a sketch, and estimate fabric
needs to save you from over or
underbuying. Prices are flexible:
she can work to a fixed budget (for
wedding dresses for example) or
you can negotiate a price based on
design, size, complexity etc. A
speciality is maternity wedding
dresses (making the least of what
you've got); she will also make up
your commercial patterns in your
own fabric and adjust them to fit
you perfectly. Prices from about
£45.00 for this service.

KENT

BECKENHAM

MADEMOISELLE
216 High Street
Beckenham
081 650 4326

Open: 9.30 to 5.30 Mon. to Sat.
Credit Cards: Access, American
Express, Visa

Large designer lounge in the chic
Italian style for the well-heeled
professional. Escada, Laurel,
Georges Rech, Gaston Jaunet,
Crisca all arranged in collections.
Evening wear from Frank Usher,
John Charles, Bellville Sassoon,
Bernshaw. Swimwear by Gottex.
Full range of Stephen Collins belts.
Plenty of seats for waiting friends,
five large changing rooms, sizes 8
to 18 and an alteration service.
Prices start at £100.00;
sophisticated staff.

GREATER LONDON

EDGWARE

HARPERS
11 The Promenade
Station Road
Edgware
081 958 6465

Open: 9.00 to 5.30 Mon. to Fri; 9.30 to 6.00 Sat.
Credit Cards: Access, American Express, Diners Club, Visa

Minimal chic haunt for the professional fashion shopper. Mostly wearable expensive classics for the wealthy well dressed thirty plus. Clothes in colour coded groups, with the very expensive designers (Ozbek, Myrène de Prémonville) in splendid isolation. Also a good range of 'bread and butter' labels for everyday wear. Even so, prices range from £45.00 to £600.00. Sizes 8 to 16, but particularly strong in the smaller sizes. Also shoes, boots and accessories.

ENFIELD

FRED & GINGER
8a Southbury Road
Enfield Town
081 366 2991

Open: 10.00 to 5.30 Mon. and Tue; 10.00 to 6.00 Thurs. to Sat; closed on Wed.
Credit Cards: Access, American Express, Diners Club, Visa

Tiny intimate comfortable shop – almost like shopping in someone's front room. Extremely personal service. Mostly smart casuals, but individuality is assured by only stocking each item in three sizes. Interesting labels: Christian Lacroix, Emmanuelle Khan, Marilla Burani; Paloma Picasso sunglasses and yummy costume jewellery. Regular customers are on the mailing list, so are forewarned about the new seasons designs and get priority in the sales January/February and August/September. Sizes 8 to 16, prices from £50.00 to £600.00.

HARROW

ABONNE
Station Road
Harrow
081 427 7142

Open: 10.00 to 6.00 Mon. to Sat.
Credit Cards: Access, American Express, Diners Club, Visa

Seductive window display for small shop which specialises in glitzy designer separates this side of outrageous. Mixture of labels, including own (Abonné). Friendly welcoming staff who have made the amazing discovery that not all women have perfect figures, and who will help you put a look together. Not for the young and fragile: fun clothes for grown up working women with Rock Princess yearnings in them. Sizes 8 to 14, prices £50.00 to £300.00.

SURREY

FARNHAM

KATIE JAMES
37–38 Downing Street
Farnham
0252 722537

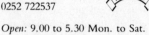

Open: 9.00 to 5.30 Mon. to Sat.
Credit Cards: Access, American
Express, Diners Club, Visa

Lovely spacious carpeted shop,
comfy chairs, marble topped tables
and jardinieres. Friendly helpful
staff, clothes in well grouped
displays; small exquisite lingerie
section, also swimwear.
Occasionally shoes if they are part
of an outfit. Great evening wear.
Good selection of Mondi, Escada
and Yarell and similar labels in sizes
8 to 20. Wonderful Italian
seamstress on the premises for
alterations. Although main
collection is obviously for
professional thirtysomethings
(prices from £80.00 to £800.00/
£900.00) there is also a jolly range
of younger casuals in bold bright
prints. Their sales are knockout –
real reductions and no bought-in
tat: queues round the block and
'changing on the stairs it gets so
full' (there are seven changing
rooms).

GODALMING

THISLEY TEXTILE
DESIGNS
1 Mousehill Lane
Milford
Godalming GU8 5BH
048 68 24769

Open: 10.00 to 5.30 Mon. to Sat.
Credit Cards: Access, Visa

Not at first glance a fashion hunting
ground: basically a woven textile
showcase – lots of wall hangings,
rugs and meditation shawls (have
one made up in your own auric
colours); they also have weaving
classes. Worth rooting round in
(there's a box of toys to distract the
tinies); rather magic woven cloaks,
unusual jackets (£68.00 to £175.00),
local hand knits (£30.00 to £60.00).
Very individual clothes for people
who really know their own style
and how to experiment with it.

GUILDFORD

VIVIENNE SMITH
SIMPLY CLOTHES
73a North Street
Guildford
0483 63645

Open: 9.00 to 5.30 Mon. to Sat.
Credit Cards: Access, American
Express, Diners Club, Visa

Own label cotton dresses, soft
suits, long and short taffeta party
frocks all at sensible prices. For
more details see page 29. There are
also branches at BATH, BRISTOL,

HULL, LEEDS, NOTTINGHAM, SHEFFIELD, WAKEFIELD and YORK.

Special Sizes

OPINIONS
103 Woodbridge Road
Guildford
0483 33304

Open: 9.30 to 5.00 Mon. to Sat.
Credit Cards: Access, American Express, Visa

Branch of the splendid OPINIONS chainette. Proper clothes for career women who break the mould. Big is Beautiful, Hesselhoj, Steel and Reeves etc. and own label Original Opinions. Sizes 16 to 30, prices from £20.00 to £450.00. There are other Opinions in BRIGHTON (flagship store) and CANTERBURY.

OXTED

CHANTERELLE
113 Station Road East
Oxted RM8 0QE
0883 714389

Open: 9.30 to 5.30 Mon. to Sat.
Credit Cards: Access, Visa

Bright, good-looking with a full selection of UK and euro clothes; great range of Ports International natural fabric classics, Le Truc and Tru tailored separates and blouses, Jacques Vert, Alain Cannelle. Well cut special occasion wear from Irish designer Michel Ambers and Kasper for A.S.L, a collection from America. Very strong on evening separates (range expands enormously during the Christmas season: they know how to live in Surrey). Fine selection of shoes and hats to complete the look. Sizes 10 to 16, prices affordable (£24.00 to £130.00). Friendly, personal service. Down the road is a younger sister shop NOUVELLE carrying sportier casual fashion (See below).

NOUVELLE
83 Station Road East
Oxted RH8 0QE
0883 715659

Open: 9.30 to 5.30 Mon. to Sat.
Credit Cards: Access, American Express, Diners Club, Visa

A branch of CHANTERELLE just up the road; for sportier, more casual (and less expensive) taste. Mexx separates, swimwear and accessories, surfies Ocean Pacific; interesting range of inexpensive, high quality mix and match casuals from Canada under the Tabby label, fun Cinch clothes and printed French cottons from Tilber. Sizes 10 to 14/16.

WEYBRIDGE

Lingerie

TEMPTATIONS
14 Baker Street
Weybridge KT13 8AU
0932 842207

Open: 9.30 to 5.30 Mon. to Sat.
Credit Cards: Access, American
Express, Visa

Branch of the Wimbledon
Temptations. Lingerie experts
selling La Perla and interesting
swimwear including Robbie
Cranfield, the sophisticated face of
Ken Done.

Shoes and Leather

ACCENT
63–65 Queens Road
Weybridge KT13 9UQ
0932 841936

Open: 9.30 to 5.30 Mon. to Sat.
Credit Cards: Access, American
Express, Diners Club, Visa

Ferragamo shoes without the
bother of Bond Street; this tranquil
pink and grey shop carries a full
range of Ferragamo (the wonderful
man who thought every woman
should be shod like a princess)
shoes, which magically seem to fit
every foot in maximum comfort.
Also Ferragamo scarves and
shawls; Jourdan and Bally (not the
chain store range). Sizes 3 to 8,
widths B and C. Prices start about
£40.00 for Bally up to £135.00 for
Ferragamo. Great selection of
costume jewellery from Yves St
Laurent, Christian Dior at the top
end to wonderful Butler &
Wilsonesque things from Barbara
Easton. No more David Shilling
millinery extravaganzas, but
special occasion hats can be made to
order by Margaret Partington (you
can also hire from her). First class
unobtrusive service from friendly
staff is seducing more and more
customers from London.

PERIA
Waterloo Terrace
Baker Street
Weybridge
0932 852048

Open: 9.30 to 5.30 Mon. to Sat.
Credit Cards: Access, American
Express, Diners Club, Visa

Exclusive, own label Italian shoes
in a warm wonderful shop in the
Tuscan style (gleaming dark wood,
chandeliers). Specialize in exotic
leathers – lizard, crocodile, ultra
supple calf – and make shoes in
classic lasting styles. They have
shops in Italy, but this is the
exclusive outlet in England. Sizes
35 to 41, expect to pay from £60.00
to £400.00 (for crocodile). Co-
ordinating handbags, organisers
and other leather goods for that
enviable Milan total chic. They also
make own design leather clothes to
order; you choose what kind and
colour of leather you want.
Trousers from about £250.00, also
suits and dresses. Menswear and
shoes also sold.

LONDON

• • • • • • • • • •

London without tears; take it in villages:
Camden for the bohemian stylist;
Hampstead and Highgate for design on
Sundays; Islington for radical chic;
Richmond, Twickenham and Barnes for
independent dressing; offbeat ethnicity
from Portobello; the best of the central
indies. Plus a review of the Big Guns and
selection from the frontline designers.

LONDON CENTRAL

BIG SHOPPING

For the timid, department stores offer an easy way to shop; the best of the big guns are given below.

....

DICKINS & JONES
Regent Street
London W1
071 734 7070

Open: 9.00 to 6.00 Mon. to Sat; late (8.00) Thurs.
Credit Cards: Access, American Express, Diners Club, Visa; Dickins & Jones Account

Restaurants; lavatories; hair salon

Probably the best of the House of Fraser stores; who else greets you with a tuxedoe'd smoothie tinkling the ivories of a cream grand piano and crooning agreeable tunes from yesteryear? Four floors of fashion, rather tiring to cover in one day. Strong on the mid label range, helpful and knowledgeable staff, excellent alteration service. Good accessories but they are rather too far away from the clothes. Regular fashion shows held in the restaurant. Not as trendy as Fenwicks, as grand as Harrods or as sophisticated as Harvey Nichols, but excellent for mid range very wearable clothes.

....

FENWICKS
New Bond Street
London W1A 3BS
071 629 9161

Open: 9.30 to 5.30 Mon. to Sat; late (7.30) Thurs.
Credit Cards: Access, American Express, Visa; Fenwicks Account Card

Restaurant; lavatories; hair salon

Flagship of the Fenwicks Empire (see NEWCASTLE), one of the best stores for young, well priced fashion as well as all the main labels: Farhi, InWear, Penny Black, Mondi, Betty Jackson, Paul Costelloe etc: particularly strong on hats and accessories; good department for larger sizes (Size Up Collections – Marina Rinaldi, Patrizia, Persona). Rather a haphazard layout, with many changes of level for the unwary.

Other Fenwicks at Leicester, Brent Cross, Newcastle on Tyne, Oxford, Windsor and Canterbury.

....

HARRODS
Knightsbridge
London
SW1
071 730 1234

Open: 9.00 to 6.00 Mon. to Sat; 9.30 to 7.30 Wed.
Credit Cards: All

Restaurants; coffee shop; lavatories

Omnia omnibus ubique: everything for everybody everywhere. That is the Harrods motto, and they certainly live up to it. You can get anything at all here;

just wandering through the sheer abundance of it all is enough to make you tired. Not so fine honed, fashion wise as Harvey Nichols, but still acres of choice (from Christian Lacroix to Ballantyne, plus excellent own label stuff); punchy young department (Way In) tucked away in the penthouse. By carrying so much, they ensure that you will find something to suit your taste, dimensions and pocket. Their sale (January) is almost a blood sport.

HARVEY NICHOLS
109–125 Knightsbridge
London SW1
071 235 5000

Open: 9.00 to 6.30 Mon. to Sat; late (8.00) Thurs.
Credit Cards: American Express, Diners Club, Visa; Harvey Nichols Account

Restaurants; coffee shop; lavatories

Probably the best department store for clothes, certainly the most fashion focussed. Intelligent buying policy, everything beautifully displayed; shop here for Bruce Oldfield, Cerruti, Complice, Dolce & Gabbana, Sonia Rykiel, Armani, Ralph Lauren and, exclusively, Calvin Klein. Dinny Hall jewellery, and small Mulberry shop within a shop. Even the less expensive things are wonderful in here: particularly strong on accessories, hats, bags, belts jewellery. A delight to go in: almost as cheering as three weeks in the Seychelles.

LIBERTY
Regent Street
London W1
071 734 1234

Open: 9.00 to 6.30 Mon. to Sat; late (8.00) Thurs.
Credit Cards: Access, American Express, Diners Club, Visa; Liberty Credit Card

Restaurants; coffee shop; lavatories

Unlike any other department store in London: a great black and white tudor cottage crouching in the midst of the west end. The spirit of Arthur Liberty, intrepid importer of eastern delights, and the Arts & Crafts movement hangs elusively in the air: the great dark oak staircases, the distinct oriental slant to the accessories, the bolts of rich cloth gleaming in the reverentially dim lighting. Labyrinthine layout means you stumble on departments unexpectedly. Not the best place for high fashion shopping, but lots of lovely own label clothes made from beautiful Liberty wools and lawns, and at just about affordable prices. Great accessories, decorated with distinctive Liberty prints, and of course wonderful scarves in cotton, wool, silk etc – they sell over 13 milesworth a day. Lots of costume jewellery from young designers. Just round the corner at the uncontaminated end of Carnaby Street is a self contained shop for young fashion separates and fun hats.

GALWAY BOY
····

At the Mornington Crescent end of Camden Town is an intriguing shop, Danlann de Bairead; this is the studio and workshop of *Slim Barrett*, the Irish designer/sculptor whose fascinating jewellery was the sensation of 1989's Clothes Show. Using unusual material – lots of metal, brass, bronze, copper, glass, chainmail, Barrett's work is poetic and mysterious – celtic twilight solidified. Remote barbarian gold metal breast plates, brass and glass crucifixes, lots of constellation imagery: his starry necklaces and brooches make you look as if you have brushed through distant galaxies. Not cheap (starting price around £50.00) but you are buying a piece of art.

····

Danlann de Bairead
72d Crowndale Road
London NW1
071 387 6419

Open 10.00 to 7.00 Mon. to Sat. or ring for an appointment.

····

NORTH LONDON

CAMDEN

DUDU
95 Parkway
London NW1
071 267 1097

Open: 9.30 to 5.30 Mon. to Sat.
Credit Cards: Access, American Express, Diners Club, Visa

Hopeless parking

Lovely friendly comfortable little shop up near Regent's Park; lots of wood and rickety stairs to the basement (don't worry, they've stood the test of time). Bright casual clothes, little plain suits, lots of 'one size' clothes; French Connection, Sun & Sand and loose 'indiany' cottons. The changing rooms are rather rugged, but the staff are friendly and helpful, and prices are very affordable to acceptable. Clothes are packed on racks and you can have great fun searching through them. Also colourful eccentric shoes, knitwear, coloured tights, some period clothes. Attracts lots of interesting Camden originals (artists, actors, musicians). Very jolly antidote to high profile label shopping. There is another branch at 171 Finchley Road, NW3.

Knitwear

MUIR & OSBORNE
138 Regent's Park Road
London NW1 8XL
071 722 2597

Open: 10.30 to 6.00 Tues. to Sat;
closed Mon.
Credit Cards: Access, Visa

Very attractive shop, much painted
wood (including the floor), Alice in
Wonderland fantasy furniture, lots
of decorative objects, china and
fabric to delight the eye. Beautiful
hand made patterned knitwear
from size tiny (children) upwards
and costing £60.00 to £300.00.
Wearable by the discerning of all
ages, but great fans among the
media folk and well-to-do arties.
Friendly, welcoming staff/owners.

Dressing Up

ESCAPADE
150 Camden High Street
London NW1
071 485 7384

Open: 10.00 to 7.00 Mon. to Fri;
10.00 to 6.00 Sat.
Credit Cards: Access, Visa

What daftness is this? Costume
foolery: life enhancing shop hiring
out all manner of cunning disguises
to enliven parties, stag do's, office
wakes etc – everything from Guy
the Gorilla to Chicken Little.
Wacky lot, these NW1ers. Expect
to pay from £15.00 and a £20.00
deposit.

CAMDEN LOCK MARKET
····
Camden Lock,
Chalk Farm Road
London NW1
····
Saturdays and Sundays
····
Always a good haunt for
unusual jewellery, outré
design and period/antique
clothes, Camden Lock
market has now burst out
of the Lock and sprawls
southwards down Chalk
Farm Road to Camden
Town tube station.
Fight your way over to the
patch near the canal for
original hand made clothes,
handknits etc; earring buffs
will spend hours in the
cobbled courtyard.
····
Look out for Roger Stone's
real silver earrings for under
a tenner.
····
If you are doing serious
shopping, avoid Sundays:
mass rallying of
North London's finest
fashion victims
– much strutting and posing –
makes it almost impossible
to get to the stalls.
····

HAMPSTEAD & HIGHGATE

CHARLI
31 Heath Street
Hampstead
London NW3
071 794 7998

Open: 9.30 to 5.30 Mon. to Sat.
Credit Cards: Access, American
Express, Diners Club, Visa

Relaxed shopping in pine and white
washed shop with jolly Casablanca
wooden ceiling fans. Stunning
window displays. There are four
Charlis; they all give maximum
design impact and excellent choice
without draining the bank balance:
£200.00 can make you look
megabucks. The look is based
mainly on mixing and matching
separates and the staff are very
helpful; four changing rooms, each
with own mirror, so you can get it
right in private. Sizes 8 to 14, price
range £25.00 to max. £400.00.
Labels are Ghost, French
Connection, Pamplemousse,
Twisted Sister, Nieuw Amsterdam
Peil, Exile, Extravert etc. New
stock comes in every eight weeks or
so. Also jeans and sweatshirts,
tracksuits (Bik Bok). Leather from
Forma; beaut swimwear from Ken
Done in the summer. Other Charlis
at MUSWELL HILL BROADWAY, ST
CHRISTOPHER'S PLACE SOUTHGATE
and the lower floor of the shopping
complex at Bond Street Tube
Station.

DESIGNS
60 Rosslyn Hill
London NW3
071 435 0100

Open: 10.00 to 5.45 Mon. to Sat;
late (7.45) Thurs.
Credit Cards: Access, Visa

The worst kept best kept secret in
northwest London: cheap(er) chic.
Friendly staff help you look
stunning for less with immaculate
second hand designer labels;
Valentino, Kenzo, Byblos and
many others; Chanels have been
known. Sizes are mainly 10 to 12,
prices naturally vary. It pays to
keep an eagle eye on this one: on
Saturday afternoon it's a well-bred
scrum down.

DUO
16 Upper Kingswell Centre
Heath Street
Hampstead
London NW3
071 435 0770

Open: 10.00 to 6.00 Mon. to Sat;
1.00 to 6.00 SUNDAY
Credit Cards: Access, American
Express, Diners Club, Visa

Marble, limed oak and chrome;
very jolly young staff and youthful
designs from Fabrice Karel, Lolita
Lempicka Bis, Soap Studio,
SportMax in sizes 8 to 14. Their
own knitwear (DUO); swimwear
from the presumptive Mrs Jagger.
Prices from £50.00 to £300.00

EBENEZER MISSION
67 Highgate High Street
London N6
081 347 9409

Open: 10.00 to 5.30 Mon. to Thurs;
10.00 to 6.00 Fri. and Sat; 11.00 to
4.00 SUNDAY
Credit Cards: None

Parking dreadful

Small double fronted ex-mission
(surprise surprise); lovely friendly
people who design and make their
own clothes: high octane, eclectic,
unusual design: upmarket 50esque
clothes a speciality. Sizes 8 to 16. If
you like a design but it is too short/
long/whatever, they will make up
one to fit you: they will also make
clothes to your own specs: £30.00
to £400.00, but loaded with
distinctive style. Bargains at sale
time (January and summer). Off
beat wedding outfits also made.

....

NICOLE FARHI
27 Hampstead High Street
London NW3
071 435 0866

Open: 9.30 to 5.30 Mon. to Sat.
Credit Cards: Access, American
Express, Diners Club, Visa

Hopeless parking

Showcase for the Nicole Farhi
collection of cool, plain, beautiful
clothes that make you feel a million
dollars. Shop style (three floors)
equally cool and understated.
Obviously almost a shrine for the
Farhi addict, and the place for the
whole range. Great clothes, shame

about the staff, who are rather
snooty and intimidating. Sizes are 8
to 14, and alterations available if
you dare ask. You may feel better
buying your Farhi at Harrods or
Harvey Nichols. Prices begin at
around £100.00. There are also
Nicole Farhi shops at 193 Sloane
Street, SW1, 25–26 St
Christopher's Place, London W1
and in MANCHESTER.

....

KUMAGAI
58 Rosslyn Hill
Hampstead
London NW3
071 431 3547

Open: 10.00 to 6.00 Mon. to Sat;
12.00 to 5.00 SUNDAY
Credit Cards: Access, Visa

No-nonsense chic in large(ish) glass
and wood shop. Betty Jackson,
OuiSet and the like in sizes 8 to 14.
Good pit stop for busy dressers
about to move over to the fast lane.

....

SUNDAY CHIC
····
If the urge for a frock should
overcome you on Sunday,
shops in the Hampstead fashion
triangle (Kingswell Centre,
Heath Street and Rosslyn Hill)
are open on Sunday afternoons.
····
See individual shops for times.
····

SURPLUS REQUIREMENTS

····

Every ten years or so, a new generation 'discovers' Laurence Corner, purveyor of cheap offbeat chic, and Vogue models are photographed looking sulky in sailor suits.

····

It's a great shop: all the stock is ex-service surplus; you can pick up very sexy pants (ex French Navy); Biggles flying suits; American leather flying jackets; Out of Africa shorts and all manner of jolly accessories for not very much money.

····

Clever button swapping could build you the Mondi matelot look for a quarter of the price.

····

**Laurence Corner
62–64 Hampstead Road
London NW1**
071 388 6811

····

**VIEW
17–18 Upper Kingswell Centre
Heath Street
London NW3 1EN**
071 435 2995

Open: 10.00 to 6.00 Mon. to Sat;
12.30 to 6.00 SUNDAY
Credit Cards: Access, American Express, Diners Club, Visa

Very design oriented, terminally chic temple of fashion (slate floor, black on black, chrome etc) with equally excruciatingly cred labels: Myrène de Prémonville, Sophie Sitbon (Kenzo for the chaps). Women's clothes upstairs, men below. Do not be frightened: grown up, intelligent staff very helpful and informed, understand their regulars' lifestyles very well, and welcome new and occasional customers. Prices range from £20.00 to £450.00. Sizes are 10 to 14, alterations for a small fee. Another View in RICHMOND.

Bags & Accessories

**TANNERS
23 High Street
Hampstead
London NW1**
071 431 1572

Open: 9.30 to 6.00 Mon. to Sat.
Credit Cards: Access, American Express, Diners Club, Visa

Splendid friendly shop selling own label all leather bags and shoes, jolly Fred Bare hats and stylish jewellery. See RICHMOND.

Dress Hire

THE FROCKERY
78 Fortune Green Road
London NW6
071 433 1714

Open: 10.00 to 6.30 Mon. to Sat.
Credit Cards: Access, Visa

Fool the world with a scrummy party frock or ballgown hired from The Frockery. Huge range to choose from, including some young designer one-offs. If you like what you borrow too much to part with it, they will sell it (or one like it) to you. Hire prices range from £30.00 to £100.00; expect to pay £60.00/£70.00 on average.

Jewellery

BRANCHE
41 St John's Wood High Street
London NW8 7NJ
071 586 8638

Open: 10.00 to 6.00 Mon. to Sat.
Credit Cards: Access, American Express, Diners Card, Visa

Wonderfully deco reseda green and gold shop selling chunky and unusual gilt jewellery from France; tiny porcelain shoes from Florence to store your rings in; sensationally delectable suede bejewelled gloves from America: £150.00 a pair, but so decadent. All purchases are gift wrapped in Branché green and gold wooden boxes. Prices start at £25.00/£30.00.

XYZ
74 Heath Street
London NW3
071 794 3242

Open: 10.00 to 6.00 Mon. to Sat; 12.00 to 5.00 SUNDAY
Credit Cards: Access, American Express, Transax, Visa

Good fun in this small friendly shop; intriguing jumbly eclectic decor: hand-daubed walls, 1920s cabinets, romantic old trunks and cabin luggage, traditional kelims (these are for sale) make a great foil to the large range of modern costume jewellery: glitzy Chantal, Atelier, Pellini from Italy, Reminiscence, Glynneth Barren, and major bead man Eric Beamon. Something to suit everybody's tastes, and prices ranging from £12.00 to £300.00, although E. Beamon sometimes reaches more stratospheric levels. You can have your jewellery repaired here. Hats from Fred Bare, and a small range of separates for men and women (size 8 to 14): Betty Jackson, The Shirtmaker, Extravert, Cream Tea, and own label (XYZ). Really an extremely agreeable shop to be in: staff relaxed and make you feel totally at ease. There is a second XYZ at 76 Wells Street London W1.

ISLINGTON

CLUSAZ
56 Cross Street
London N1
071 359 5596

Open: 10.30 to 6.30 Mon. to Sat.
Credit Cards: Access, American
Express, Diners Club, Visa

Cool, quiet grown up shop with
alluring window displays. Chic,
together clothes from WilliWear,
Fenn, Wright & Manson, InWear
and the like. Also Clusaz own label
designer casuals. Sizes 10 to 14, and
prices from good value to
expensive – suits can rack up to
£250.00; good sale reductions in
January. Excellent changing rooms
with huge mirrors. Good selection

GILL WING
· · · ·
The most unlikely place for
wacky costume jewellery is a
tiny shop – more of a cupboard
with ambitions – which opens
onto Upper Street, the
Boul' Mich' of Islington. Gill
Wing is in fact three shops: an
arty kitchen shop (the
background decor of teapots are
sadly not for sale), a shopful of
daft prezzies and in between
(number 194) the tiny jewel
box, crammed to bursting with
bangles and beads, ethnic
bodywear, chunky costume
jewellery, giant rings. Great for
stylish magpies: prices vary
wildly: from £3.00 to £60.00.
· · · ·

---

of costume jewellery, hats and
accessories. Very civilized, calming
place to buy clothes: friendly,
helpful owners who offer wine to
regular customers at the end of a
hard day's shop.

DIVERSE
286 Upper Street
London N1
071 359 0081

Open: 11.00 to 7.00 Mon. to Fri;
10.30 to 7.00 Sat.
Credit Cards: Access, American
Express, Visa

Dreadful parking

Small shop with Quaker(ish) decor
owned and run by friendly,
approachable Gabrielle and Clare
Parker. Clothes to live and work in:
Soap Studio, Sara Sturgeon
Clothing, Ghost, Et Vous;
speciality is their own label big,
baggy T-shirts (hooded this
season), from £15.00. Very laid-
back shop; the decorative ethnic
jewellery and ceramics are all for
sale. Living up to its name, Diverse
intrigues all sorts of people . . . some
'Stenders shop here. And you can
get a haircut downstairs.

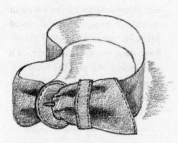

Accessories

DESIGN ALSO
101 St Paul's Road
Highbury
London N1 2NA
071 354 0035

Open: 10(ish) to 7(ish) Mon. to Sat.
Credit Cards: Mastercard, Visa

Owner Yvonne Lyddon decamped
from Hyper Hyper two years ago
to this double fronted shop in leafy
Highbury, where she sells the
biggest selection of tights and
stockings in the Western
hemisphere: and not a trace of
American Tan to be seen. All
makes of hosiery, all unusual –
hand printed tights from £11.00 to
£21.00. Sizes small, average and
tall. All the socks in the world here
too. On the lower floor is lingerie
(Warners, Fantasie, Andrea Paul,
handmade undies from Bloomers).
No one is allowed out of the shop
unless their new bra fits perfectly –
sizes 32 to 38, cups a to f. Silk and
cotton underwear made to order.
Boggling selection of costume
jewellery: everything from glass
and diamante to heavy metal, from
30 different makers; lots of young
new designers. A crystal necklace
will set you back £100.00, but
earrings start from £4.75 (and go on
to £50.00). Also lovely individual
belts, curved and shaped; lots of
hats; hand-painted scarves. And if
you cannot face the mirror of a
morning, you can buy beautiful
masks – papier mâché at £85.00,
metal £57.00 to £65.00.

Antique & Period Clothing

ANNIE'S
Camden Passage
Islington N1

Open: 9.00 to 6.00 Wed. and Sat.
(market days); 11.00 to 5.30 rest of
week (not Sun).
Credit Cards: Visa

Tiny little shop in the centre of
Camden Passage, the centre of
antique trade in the celebrated
Camden Passage market. Annie's
has been here for years. Venerable
building full of sensational antique
lace, beaded and sequinned jackets,
silk day dresses, shoes occasionally,
and belts. Naturally, stock changes
all the time, so you have to strike
regularly. Sizes about 8 to 14(ish).
A 1920s beaded jacket will cost
around £200.00, but you can get
day jackets for £20.00 or so and
evening jackets for £50.00.
Alterations possible. Antique
wedding dresses start around
£145.00. They also sell lace in
lengths, and can make it up to your
requirements: pretty little cotton
lawn and lace tops for about £45.00.
Have a care in the changing room: it
is minuscule, and separated from
the shop window by a mere curtain
– an unthinking gesture could
display your all to passers by. You
may end up in a Japanese holiday
snap album.

Jewellery

VERTU
63 Cross Street
London N1
071 226 7317

Open: 12.00 to 6.00 Tue. to Thurs.
Credit Cards: Access, American
Express, Diners Club, Visa

Opposite Clusaz (see page 94);
unusual 1930s and 1940s jewellery
from Germany, France and
America.
    Copper and enamel, paste and
bakelite a speciality. Prices range
from £12.00 (bakelite dress clips) to
£150.00 for Weimar Republic paste
jewellery.

Knitwear

MELINDA COSS   ARCHERS
1 Copenhagen Street
London N1
071 833 3929

Open: 10.00 to 5.30 Mon. to Fri;
only open on Sat. from mid
October to February
Credit Cards: Access, American
Express, Visa

Not actually a shop, more a
showcase for samples of Melinda
Coss designs; truly wondrous
woollies – jackets and sweaters –
that can be made to order from their
pattern book. All natural fibres
(shetland, lambswool, silk, cotton,
mohair, alpaca); sizes 12 to 16(ish).
Prices range from £50.00 to £150.00
At the end of the season (January)

lucky people may snap up a one-off
sample. Showroom is strong on the
ovine theme: a flock of wooden
sheep (real wool fleeces) graze
contentedly therein. They are also
for sale.

Party Frocks

COCKTAIL
206 Upper Street
Islington
London N1
071 226 9292

Open: 11.00 to 7.00 Mon. to Sat.
Credit Cards: None

Extraordinary establishment.
Glitter occasion wear, made to
measure only, but you can snap up
some bargains from one-off and
samples they occasionally sell.
Only for the bold, famous or rich
and daft. Shiny fabrics, leathers,
suede, silk, much glitz – they do a
roaring trade for TV and theatrical
occasions and in America.
Cheapest frock is £150.00 and it
tops out around £1000.00, but
every one is an original (you can
present your own design or they
will design for you). Inside the shop
is like a theatre wardrobe, tailor's
dummies in the backroom etc.
Rather intimidating in its way, but
if you are upfront enough to wear
what's on show then going in to
look will be a mere bagatelle. You
will also be able to cope with genius
proprietor Malcolm Hall, who can
be brusque on occasion.

KILBURN

Shoes

CINZIA
157 Kilburn High Road
London NW6
071 328 8534

Open: 9.30 to 6.00 Mon. to Sat.
Credit Cards: Access, American
Express, Diners Club, Visa

A find. Small, smart shop that sells
classic Italian leather shoes for at
least £10.00 less than West End
prices. For example, soft glacé
leather pumps cost around £35.00;
leather bootees around £50.00.
Sizes 3 to 7/8, mostly medium to
narrow fittings. Great sales
(January and July). Men's shoes
too.

....

KRISP
97 Kilburn High Road
London NW6
071 624 3853

Open: 9.30 to 6.00 Mon. to Sat.
Credit Cards: Access, Visa

Smallish fun shop; v. good prices
for snappy young own label
separates: wool and cotton feature;
also suits. Reasonable street chic for
the 16s to 25s. Great for jeans.

....

MUSWELL HILL & SOUTHGATE

CHARLI
The Broadway
Muswell Hill N10
081 883 9151

Open: 10.00 to 6.00 Mon. to Sat.
Credit Cards: Access, American
Express, Diners Club, Visa

One of the four Charlis; clothes for
maximum design impact and
excellent choice without draining
the bank balance: £200.00 can make
you look megabucks. The look is
based mainly on mixing and
matching separates. See
HAMPSTEAD & HIGHGATE. Also
Charlis at ST CHRISTOPHER'S PLACE,
SOUTHGATE and the lower floor of
the Bond Street Tube.

....

CHARLI
St Christopher's Place
Southgate
London N14
081 882 4702

Open: 10.00 to 6.00 Mon. to Sat.
Credit Cards: Access, American
Express, Diners Club, Visa

Another of the four Charlis; clothes
for maximum design impact and
excellent choice without draining
the bank balance: £200.00 can make
you look megabucks. See
HAMPSTEAD & HIGHGATE. Also
Charlis at MUSWELL HILL
BROADWAY and the lower floor of
the Bond Street Tube Station
shopping complex.

....

FROCKS AWAY
79–85 Fortis Green Road
Muswell Hill Road
London N10
081 444 9309

Open: 9.30 to 5.30 Mon. to Sat.
Credit Cards: Access, Visa

Totally magnificent shop.
Upmarket but v. friendly –
stripped floors, plants, terracotta
busts; extremely interesting clothes
– Twisted Sister, I'm No Painted
Canvas, Capital, Et Vous as well as
classic Nicole Farhi, casual Oilily
etc. Sizes 8 to 16 (alterations
available) prices £15.00 (T-shirt) to
£250.00 (silk trousers). Amazing
jewellery from Malcolm Morris
and Dan Drew. Wonderful
ambience, great service; huge
clientele from North London
theatricals (Maureen Lipman,
Emily Lloyd, Phyllis Logan,
Frances Tomelty, Alison
Steadman) and the rock folk who
frequent Dave 'Eurythmics'
Stewart's local recording studio
(Feargal Sharkey, Gary Kemp, Mrs
Wyman). Next door is Early

Clothing, part of Frocks Away
selling clothes for junior groovers.
They have videos, books and toys
to entertain the young idea so that
you can do some serious frocking.

NOTTING HILL

ALBERRE ODETTE
39/41 Porchester Road
London W2 5DP
071 229 4814/727 7676

Open: 9.00 to 6.00 Mon. to Sat; late
(7.30) Fri.
Credit Cards: Access, Visa

Gem of a local shop selling high
power labels at below high street
prices: Karl Lagerfeld, Bellville
Sassoon, L'Estelle, Synonyme for
example. Also growing range of
own label designer clothes,
focusing on evening wear.
Excellent alteration service. Sizes 8
to 16, prices £50.00 to £500.00.
Great sales (December and July)
with 50% off. Wardrobe planning
advice; good quality unusual
accessories (hats, jewellery, shoes
etc). Strong local following.

PORTOBELLO MARKET
· · · ·
Portobello Road
London W2
· · · ·
Still zany after all these years:
best clothes bargains to be had
early on Friday and Saturday
mornings under the flyover,
before the tourists get up.
· · · ·

Hats

PORCHESTER HATS
4 Porchester Place
London W2
071 402 1254

Open: 10.00 to 6.00 Mon. to Fri;
10.00 to 1.00 Sat.
Credit Cards: Access, American
Express, Visa

Elegant shop: all cream walls,
antique screens, full length mirrors
and lovely classical music.
Wonderful colour-themed window
display, changed weekly. Hats
from the big leaguers: Stephen
Jones, Freddie Fox, Gabriela
Ligenza, Siggi, Andrew Wilkie.
Prices range from £28.00 to
£350.00. Also a good selection of
hair ornaments for the hat-phobic.
A particularly sound wheeze is the
changing rooms provided so you
can try on important hats with the
outfit you intend to wear with
them. You can also hire hats here.

KIRSTEN WOODWARD
26 Portobello Green Arcade
281 Portobello Road
London W10
081 960 0090

Open: 9.30 to 5.30 Mon. to Sat.
(knock if the door is closed)
Credit Cards: None

It's certainly different in here; the
shop is convinced that it's an
African king's royal hut: textured
daub walls, straw roof and floor,
and shell encrusted fake leopard
skin settees. Good fun atmosphere;
the hats made by Woodward are all
unique but wearable – materials
include leather, suede, fake fur.
Prices from £30.00 to £300.00; a
cheaper range – KW – is also
available. Hats come in s,m or l
sizes, and can be altered if
necessary. Fashion media persons
love Woodward hats; and they are a
wow with Japanese tourists. You
can also buy a limited range in
Harvey Nichols and Liberty, but
it's not nearly so much fun as
coming here.

Jewellery

FRONTIERS
39 Pembridge Road
London W11
071 727 6132

Open: 11.00 to 6.30 Mon. to Sat.
Credit Cards: Access, American
Express, Diners Club, Visa

Great shop for ethnic jewellery.
Most of it is from the Middle East
and Asia; antique pieces from
Morocco, Thailand and Yemen;
intricate coral and black beaded
ropes from Afghanistan; modern
pieces from India. None of it is
cheap: but it is all redolent of the
romance of exotic places. Throw a
sop to your wanderlust with a pair
of earrings at about £18.00.
Intricate necklaces can cost up to
£450.00.

COVENT GARDEN

DROOPY & BROWNS
99 St Martin's Lane
LONDON WC2
071 379 4514

Open: 10.00 to 6.00 Mon. to Sat.
Credit Card: Access, American
Express, Diners Club, Visa

London arm of the shop that started
life in York. Gorgeous own label
party frocks and separates. Sizes 10
to 16, prices reasonable to
expensive. Other Droopys in
BATH, EDINBURGH, YORK.

....

KOKO
4 Garrick Street
London WC2
071 836 9511

Open: 10.30 to 7.00 Mon. to Fri;
10.30 to 6.30 Sat.
Credit Cards: Access, American
Express, Visa

Light bright hi tech deco shop;
friendly helpful staff make it a
pleasure to go in – some shops in
this area are far too stylish to be
cluttered up by mere customers.
Mostly understated and very
wearable French and Italian clothes:
Lolita Lempicka, Pierrot, Val
Piriou etc in sizes 8 to 14. Prices
range from £25.00 to £300.00.
Good sales in January and July:
some clothes less than half price.

....

Hats

THE HAT SHOP
58 Neal Street
London WC2
071 836 6718

Open: 10.00 to 6.00 Mon. to Thurs;
10.00 to 7.00 Fri; 10.00 to 5.30 Sat.
Credit Cards: Access, Visa

Arguably the shop that brought
back the hat as a fashion statement.
Immense selection of own label
hats for men and women. All sorts
of styles and a good price range: the
cheapest knockabout straw is
around £6.00; gorgeous trimmed
cartwheel is anything from
£150.00 up. Small groups of
disappointed people are often seen
clustered against The Hat Shop
window: they are not displaced
tourists; they are waiting for their
turn to go in. The small shop gets
so crowded that every now and
then one of the staff has to act as a
polite doorstop to keep the
numbers down. Excellent range of
men's felt hats, many of which are
bought by girls: they keep rain off
better than any umbrella. Helpful,
knowledgeable staff. You can have
a hat made up from your own
material. There are also Hat Shops
at 99, Gees Court, St Christopher's
Place, London W1 and in
GLASGOW.

....

Knitwear

WESTAWAY & WESTAWAY
62–65 Great Russell Street
London WC1
071 636 1718

and
92 Great Russell Street
London WC1
071 405 4479

Open: 9.00 to 5.30 Mon. to Sat.
Credit Cards: Access, American
Express, Diners Club, JCB, Visa

Splendid traditional knitwear
emporium; cashmere, shetland,
lambswool, mohair and camelhair
for women and men. Classic style
and an enormous range of sweaters,
cardigans, jackets, shawl, scarves
etc. Sizes 34 to 44 ladies.
Expensive, but you are buying an
heirloom. Also kilts, duffle coats,
raincoats, sports jackets etc in the
classic mode. A great favourite
with American tourists.

·····

Shoes

ANELLO & DAVIDE
35 Drury Lane
London WC2
071 836 1983

Open: 9.00 to 5.00 Mon. to Sat.
Credit Cards: Access, Visa

Horrific parking

Large, rather draughty shop with
long theatrical tradition (the bulk of
their trade is ballet and stage shoes).
This is where you can buy little
leather character shoes (the kind

with a strap and button that A. in
Wonderland wears in the Tenniel
drawings); originally, they were
for stage work, with steel taps in
the toes, but they have stealthily
become a fashion staple. They
come in three heel heights, any
colour you like, even two tone, and
you can have the buttons moved to
fit for a trifling sum. You can even
buy a buttonhook. Shoes sell at
about £30.00 to £40.00, half price in
the sales. Staff are wonderfully
patient and knowledgeable, even if
you are not famous (one wall of the
shop is covered with signed photos
of satisfied celebs). Their other
great speciality is dying satin shoes
to match material for ballgowns,
wedding dresses etc. It is not worth
going elsewhere: most shoe shops
that offer this service simply send
your shoes here anyway. Large
selection of white satin 'blanks' to
choose from.

·····

FASHION SCENTS
····
Penhaligon
41 Wellington Street
London WC2
071 606 5355
····
Perfumiers to the Duke of
Edinburgh also sell delightfully
unusual jewellery: tiny
perfume bottle pendants and
earrings.
····

PLUMLINE
40 Floral Street
London WC2
071 379 7856

Open: 10.30 to 6.30 Mon. to Fri;
10.00 to 6.00 Sat.
Credit Cards: Access, American
Express, Diners Club, Visa

Part of the Natural Shoe Store
group (shops at 21 Neal Street
WC2, 325 King's Road SW3 and 22
Princes Square, Glasgow). Shoes
here are well made, expensive and
worth every penny (start at around
£40.00 and stop just short of
£200.00); labels include Freelance,
Clergerie, Grenson, Vidal, Michel
Perry; sizes 36 to 41 (ladies) and 39
to 45 for men. Staff are friendly,

attentive and knowledgeable;
serious service for serious shoes.
Repairs to Plumline shoes
undertaken; they will also send
shoes by mail on request. Lots of
tourists.

Special Sizes

BASE
Rushka Murganovic
55 Monmouth Street
London WC2
071 240 8914

Open: 10.00 to 6.00 Mon. to Sat;
late (7.00) Thurs.
Credit Cards: Access, American
Express, Diners Club, Visa

Modern bright shop with a great
line in mix and match clothes for
larger sizes (14 to 28). A really
enjoyable 'shopping experience';
relaxed atmosphere, personal
service, lots of help with getting
your act together. Lovely clothes:
Givenchy, Jean Paul, Pola, Karelia,
Steel and Reeve, and own label
(Rushka Murganovic). Big belts
and big accessories to keep things in
proportion. Good range of clothes
for weddings and Ascotty
occasions. Prices range from
affordable upwards: blouses start at
£42.00, jackets at around £70.00,
skirts and trousers around £42.00,
dresses from £99.00. New stocks
come in every two or three months,
and magnificent window displays.
There is another Base in Parson's
Green (see page 116) and they are
thinking of opening more.

MUSEUM PIECES
····
For something really different,
visit your local museum.
····
The British Museum sells
handsome, well made replicas of
ancient jewellery: a pair of
Sutton Hoo earrings will set
you back about £15.00,
a torque
about £40.00.
····
For New Agers,
the Geological Museum in
South Kensington sells
jewellery
made up from real crystals
and stones.
····

W1

JANE & DADA
20 St Christopher's Place
London W1
071 486 0977

Open: 9.30 to 5.30 Mon. to Sat.
Credit Cards: Access, American
Express, Diners Club, Visa

Pedestrian zone

Smallish shop with friendly helpful
staff. Good range of uncluttered
clothes: tailored separates, good
silk blouses, interesting jumpers,
easy casuals. Most are imported
from Finland, but some of the
knitwear is English. Sizes 8 to 16,
prices acceptable to very expensive.

MARKS & SPENCER
Marble Arch
458 Oxford Street
London W1
071 935 7954

Open: 9.00 to 7.00 Mon. and Tue;
9.00 to 8.00 Wed. to Fri; 9.00 to
6.00 Sat.
Credit Cards: Own credit scheme

Well why not; Marks & Spencer
defy categorization really: not a
department store, more than a
chain store – a way of life really:
they supply one third of us with all
our underwear needs. This is the
flagship store. Vast amounts of
cashmere for the tourists and
hectares of undies (their silk ranges
are rather delicious); first with the
new ranges; some exclusives such
as suede and leathers. They are

BURLINGTON BERTIES
····

Burlington Arcade is very
upmarket and quintessentially
British: all pink and
aquamarine, it is full of
wonderful knitwear shops:
N. Peal, the cashmere kings at
no. 37; *Berk* grand slamming at
nos 6, 20 to 21 and 46;
S. Fisher at nos 22–23, selling
bright coloured hand framed
shetlands and sea island cotton
knits; and *Pickett* at no 41, with
gorgeous Georgina von Etzdorf
hand printed silk scarves,
dressing gowns, pyjamas etc;
if you leave the arcade
at the Piccadilly end,
you come out opposite
Fortnum & Mason,
possibly the most delicious
food shop in the world
(They sell clothes too.)
····

getting better at fashion – less of the
annoying motifs; they have always
had quality on their side and if you
buy judiciously and stick to basic
shapes and flexible colours, you can
build a good working wardrobe.
Everybody has shopped here at
least once in their lives: Stephen
'Hatman' Jones is bowled over by
the seaming on their men's T shirts;
Bruce Oldfield buys socks here.
Reciprocally, perhaps, the factory
that produces M & S top line
women's wear (Dewhirst) makes
Bruce's own Bruce Oldfield 1992
diffusion label.

Accessories

THE MULBERRY COMPANY
11–12 Gee's Court
St Christopher's Place
London W1M 5HQ
071 493 2547

Open: 10.00 to 6.00 Mon. to Sat;
late (7.00) Thurs.
Credit Cards: Access, American
Express, Diners Club, Visa

All delicious Mulberry products
under one modest sized roof; bags,
belts, scarves, shoes, gloves and
clothes in the distinctive style that
has 'mulberrized' most chic
wardrobes. Easy to wear, classic
British country style (most things
made in Somerset) with a fashion
twist and great range of belts,
gloves and useable bags and
baggage. It is encouraging to know
that Roger and Monty Saul (Mr &
Mrs Mulberry) dress exclusively in
Mulberry clothes and road test their
bags in real life situations.

....

```
┌─────────────────────────────────┐
│                                 │
│       PICCADILLY MARKET         │
│             ····                │
│          197 Piccadilly         │
│           London W1             │
│             ····                │
│      Fridays and Saturdays      │
│             ····                │
│    Eclectic market that is held │
│         in the forecourt of     │
│     St James church; look out for│
│       unusual ethnic jewellery. │
│             ····                │
│                                 │
└─────────────────────────────────┘
```

Jewellery

JANET FITCH

2 Percy Street
London W1
071 636 5631

Open: 10.00 to 6.00 Mon. to Sat;
late (8.00) Thurs.
Credit Cards: Access, American
Express, Diners Club, Visa

Elegant co-ordinated shop selling
clothes, jewellery, interesting
ceramics and stylish domestic
objects. Very intriguing and
innovative jewellery from such as
Eric Beamon, Wright and Teague;
young British designers actively
encouraged: for example, chrome
chunks from Michael de Nardo.
Hats from Fred Bare; women's
clothes from Betty Jackson, Planet
Earth, Rina-de-Pato (sizes 8 to 14).
Very low staff turnover,
consequently jolly, relaxed
informed staff. Even if you don't
buy anything (you can spend
anything from £20.00 to £300.00 in
here) it is life enhancing just to go
and look around it.

....

PURE FABRICATION
5 Rupert Court
London W1
071 437 1001

Open: 11.00 to 7.00 Mon. to Sat.
Credit Cards: Access, Visa

Fun jewellers in a tiny cave-like
shop; this one is really weird – great
gothic ear decor, light metallic
spirals of various sizes from
sensible to outré. And they let you

try them on. They style themselves 'jewel mongers to the fortunate'; prices are good – your ears can look really impressive for about a fiver.

Shoes

CRISPINS
28 to 30 Chiltern Street
London W1
071 486 8924

Open: 9.30 to 6.00 Mon. to Sat; late (7.00) Thurs.
Credit Cards: Access, American Express, Diners Club, Select, Visa

Specialist in narrow shoes; sizes 4 to 11 in widths AAA and AA; B and C in sizes 8 to 11. Also bags, gloves. Along the street at number 5 is Crispins Cobbler, which provides an excellent hand finished repair service for shoes, handbags and luggage. Crispins shoes can be bought by post (see page 155). There is a branch in MANCHESTER. St Crispin is the patron saint of shoemakers.

Special Sizes

KEN SMITH DESIGNS
6 Charlotte Place
London W1
071 631 3341

Open: 10.00 to 6.00 Mon. to Fri; 10.00 to 2.00 Sat.
Credit Cards: Access, American Express, Diners Club, Visa

Clothes for sizes 16+: no upper limit in height or girth. Lovely shop: white and peach and mahogany, very intimate and friendly; lots of regulars seem to use it as a sort of town club. Huge range of labels: Marimekko, Patrizia, French Vanilla, Bib, as well as own label (Ken Smith). Quite pricey (£29.00 to £700.00) but you get what you pay for. If you cannot find anything you like, they will design and make clothes to order; particularly strong on wedding dresses. They offer a jolly called a Goody Service: customers can ring up and describe the sort of clothes they are after; on supply of a credit card number or a cheque a selection will be sent by post.

Designer Shopping

The following list of designer shops has been selected on the basis of real women's experience. Even if they are beyond your purse, they are encouraging to study; all of them have welcoming, informed staff and a relaxed ambience. Some famous names have been left out, mainly because they would be inappropriate additions to a book of this nature; a few because they are so awesomely rude that you wouldn't want to spend money there even if you had it to spare.

SOUTH MOLTON MELTDOWN
····

South Molton Street is not what it was: it's looking decidedly grubby and smart money is moving elsewhere (mostly Draycott Avenue and Brompton Cross where Fulham Road becomes Brompton Road).
····
However, Browns, the shop that started it all is still there, the home of many exclusive labels expertly bought and edited by Joan Burstein: Donna Karan, Alaia Azzedine, Comme des Garçons etc.
····
The customers are equally starry –
Liza Minelli, Marie Helvin, Jacqueline Bisset, Bruce Oldfield.
····

PADDY CAMPBELL
8 Gees Court
St Christopher's Place
London W1
071 493 5646

and
17 Beauchamp Place
London SW3
071 225 0543

Open: 10.00 to 6.00 Mon. to Fri; late (7.00) Wed; 10.30 to 6.00 Sat.
Credit Cards: Access, American Express, Visa

Paddy Campbell own label clothes: stylish shirts, skirts, blouses, dresses, suits. Charming chic friendly shop, coffee served to regulars, who include Joan Collins, Diana Ross and junior royals.

ALLY CAPELLINO
95 Wardour Street
London W1
071 494 0768

Open: 10.30 to 7.00 Mon. to Fri; 11.30 to 6.00 Sat.
Credit Cards: Access, American Express, Visa

Label shopping without fear: very jolly approachable shop selling all Ally Capellino's easy, wearable clothes including the Work Wear cheapo (under £40.00) range, unavailable elsewhere. Georgina von Etzdorf scarves. Sizes 8 to 14, prices £15.00 to £1060.00. Clothes displayed in witty scenarios with props that are sold at the end of each season.

CAROLINE CHARLES
56–57 Beauchamp Place
London SW3
071 225 3197

Open: 9.30 to 5.30 Mon. to Sat.
Credit Cards: Access, American Express, Diners Club, Visa

New Caroline Charles flagship store set in elegant double fronted Georgian town house, refurbished by David Mlinaric. Inside all is light and airy: loads of fresh flowers, coffee, champagne and fizzy water offered to regular customers: offers the whole Caroline Charles collection: suits, silk dresses, formal evening wear, separates, knits, as well as menswear, bedlinens and jewellery. Sizes 8 to 14, prices affordable to very expensive.

KATHARINE HAMNETT
20 Sloane Street
London SW1
071 823 1002

Open: 9.30 to 6.00 Mon. to Sat; 10.00 to 7.00 Wed.
Credit Cards: Access, American Express, Diners Club, Visa

Katharine Hamnett main range and jeans sold (but not Hamnett II Action) in a shop impressively decorated as a scene from 20,000 Leagues under the Sea. Exceedingly helpful charming young staff. Hamnett clothes are stamped with the distinctive personality of their designer; extremely engagé and much loved by urban achievers, rock stylists and anybody not afraid to make a fashion statement. Sizing is small, medium and large and prices range from £20.00 to £1500.00. There is another Katharine Hamnett shop at 38 Princes' Square, Glasgow (041 248 3827).

MARGARET HOWELL
29 Beauchamp Place
London SW3
071 584 2362

Open: 10.00 to 6.00 Mon. to Sat.
Credit Cards: Access, American Express, Diners Club, Visa

Beautiful shop – limed oak floors, huge reassuring refectory table; beautiful clothes from Margaret Howell, comfortable, stylish, timeless British classics with a twist – intriguing fabric, imaginative stitch detailing. Expensive (trousers around £115.00) but you'll want to wear them forever.

THE WET LOOK
· · · ·
Captain O M Watts
45 Albemarle Street
London W1
· · · ·
For Swallows and Amazons: stylish souwesters, jolly matelot jerseys, shiny slickers, yottie boots and much other nautical dressing.
· · · ·

BUY DESIGN
····

Four times a year there is an unmissable frock event at Chelsea Old Town Hall. This is the Chelsea Designer Sale, when designers of all wattage sell off ends of ranges, samples, one-offs and so on; remember that their 'end-of-season' is our hot new look, as they design a season ahead. Prices are 60% of the retail price, and it is not unusual for the designers themselves to sell the clothes – buy your Workers for Freedom shirt directly from one of the Workers. For details contact **Chelsea Design Sale, 268 Lavender Hill, Battersea, London SW11 1LJ** (071 223 3706). Buy preview tickets at £5.00 per head (Access, Visa, cheque, postal orders) and pay £2.00 on the door. Upcoming sales July 27th to 29th, September 27th to 29th and December 7th to 9th. Opening hours 11.00 to 6.00 (come prepared to queue, even with your ticket) and you get a free fashion show.

····

JOSEPH
77 Fulham Road
London SW3
071 823 9500

Open: 10.00 to 6.00 Mon. to Fri; 9.30 to 6.00 Sat.
Credit Cards: Access, American Express, Diners Club, Visa

Favourite of the two flagship shops of designer lifestyle purveyor Joseph Ettedgui (the other one is at 26 Sloane Street SW1). Cool seductive, oozing with chic: the Joseph philosophy is to gather together the cream of designer clothes that you can actually look good in for longer than the statutory 15 minutes and display them so beautifully you will cry: Galliano; Ozbek, Montana, Alaia, Emma Hope shoes. You'll want all of them: get a bank loan now. Sizes 10 to 16. Rich and famous people of all ages practically live in Joseph. Joseph knitwear (jumpers, tube skirts, leggings etc) all available at Joseph Tricot shops (16 Sloane Street SW1 and 16 South Molton Street W1); Vêtements de Travail (bib and brace jeans, butch overalls in which Jean Gabin looked so intrinsically Gallic etc) available at Le Joseph (53 Kings's Road SW3).

BRUCE OLDFIELD
27 Beauchamp Place
London SW3
071 584 1363

Open: 10.00 to 6.00 Mon. to Fri; late (6.30) Wed; 11.00 to 5.30 Sat.
Credit Cards: Access, American Express, Diners Club, Visa

Very plush, comfortable and seductive shop, without affectation; exceedingly helpful staff. Totally wonderful clothes all from Bruce Oldfield; sizes 8 to 14, starting price £450.00.

Glamorous, sophisticated day and evening wear, much loved by such international stars as Charlotte Rampling, Shakira Caine, Marie Helvin. Those of us less rich and famous will turn with joy to the new Bruce Oldfield 1992 diffusion line: prices are about a third of the main collection, and the look is less celeb, more successful working girl.

....

EDINA RONAY
141 Kings Road
London SW3
071 352 1085

Open: 10.00 to 6.00 Mon. to Fri; 10.00 to 7.00 Wed; 11.00 to 6.00 Sat.

and
42 Burlington Arcade
London W1
071 495 3034

Open: 9.00 to 6.00 Mon. to Fri; 9.00 to 5.30 Sat.
Credit Cards: Access, American Express, Diners Club, Visa

The kind of clothes Patricia Hodge looks so cool and collected in: serious tailored linens, wool and gaberdine suits, wool and cashmere separates, evening wear with lots of velvet and gold lamé. Extremely chic, extremely expensive.

....

CATHERINE WALKER CHELSEA DESIGN COMPANY
65 Sydney Street
London SW3
071 352 4626

Open: 10.00 to 6.00 Mon. to Sat.
Credit Cards: Access, American Express, Diners Club, Visa

Long, lean, unfussy lines from French designer Catherine Walker; dressy daywear, wondrous ballgowns, beautiful fabric and expert cut. The Princess of Wales' favourite designer. Sizes 8 to 14; very expensive (around £900.00 for an evening dress) but the clothes last and last.

....

HYPER HYPER
· · · ·
26–40 Kensington High Street
London W8
071 938 4343
· · · ·

Hotwire your way into upfront wacky fashion by touring Hyper Hyper, a coterie of about 70 small designer outlets including stalwarts *Pink Soda,* sensible dressers *Shirley Wong,* warrior queen *Pam Hogg* and Leeds-based *Dawn Stretton,* purveyor of last seasons essential velvet shorts.
· · · ·
Noisy, hot and fun; unmissable for young smarties.
· · · ·

NEWBURGH STREET CRED

....

The smartest street in central London at the moment is little Newburgh Street. Cobbled in designer dark grey, it runs parallel to the terminally garish Carnaby Street, but is light years ahead in style terms. *John Richmond* (no. 2) currently selling rather unpleasant neo-Fascist styles; assertive warrior queen dressing from *Pam Hogg* (no. 5) jewellery from *Jess James* (no. 3) glistering against a background of tropical fish; at no. 15 the *Academy Soho* a 'Showcase for Young British Designers'. Clothes are sold under the Academy tag, with the designer's name on the other side: sharp casuals, jolly hats, fun shoes and great jewellery. Accessory kings *FFWD* have just expanded and now cover 14 and 13. Modistes *Boyd & Storey* are at no. 12 until August when it will be *Helen Storey*. On the corner of Fouberts Place is Junior Gaultier, a shrine to the *roi de bondage*. And at no. 12 Ganton Street at the other end of Newburgh is mad gothic jeweller *The Great Frog*: matt black decor, coffins, skulls; riveting collection of enamel eyeball jewellery.

....

SHIRLEY WONG
41 Old Compton Street
London W1V 5PN
071 734 6251

Open: 10.30 to 7.00 Mon. to Sat;
12.00 to 7.00 SUNDAY
Credit Cards: Access, American Express, Diners Club, Visa

Bright, classic shop selling practical, flexible smart clothes for nonsense-free working women. All Shirley Wong own label, sizes 10 to 14 (over 14s can have clothes made to measure). Expensive: starts at £115.00, but the helpful staff will advise you well, and not allow you to walk out in an unsuitable suit.

There is a Shirley Wong in Hyper Hyper (see page 109).

....

WORKERS FOR FREEDOM
4a Lower John Street
London W1
071 734 3766

Open: 9.30 to 5.30 Mon. to Sat.
Credit Cards: Access, American Express, Diners Club, Visa

Winners of 1989 British Designer of the Year Design Award, WFF are Graham Fraser and Richard Nott. Their clothes are cutting edge New Age: informal, decorative, lots of detailing, easy to wear and very expensive (the cheapest shirt is £95.00) – for successful 60s groovers who haven't forgotten how to cool out. Friendly small shop.

....

Jewellery

BUTLER & WILSON
20 South Molton Street
London W1
071 409 2955

and
189 Fulham Road
London SW3
071 352 3045

Open: 10.00 to 6.00 Mon. to Fri;
11.00 to 6.00 Sat.
Credit Cards: Access, American
Express, Diners Club, Visa

Costume jewellers to Princess of
Wales. Specializes in art nouveau
and art deco styles; when they
started out 21 years ago it was real
deco and noov, but there's simply
not enough to go round, so now
they design and make their own
silver and paste pieces, inspired by
their first love. There is also a
Butler & Wilson in GLASGOW.

....

COBRA & BELLAMY
149 Sloane Street
SW1
071 730 2823

Open: 10.30 to 6.00 Mon. to Sat.
Credit Cards: Access, American
Express, Diners Club, Visa

Exotic Cobra & Bellamy (Veronica
Manussis and Tania Hunter) sell
opulent contemporary and deco
costume jewellery; original designs
from Christopher Blum and
Barbara Bertagnolli – one-off
sterling silver, gold and gemstone
pieces; art deco watches, and
gorgeous limited edition of
glittering silver frog brooches
shimmering with onyx and lapis
lazuli; £285.00 per frog, but you can
get a pair of sterling silver earrings
for as little as £15.00.

....

HAT COUTURE
· · · ·

For the most romantic hats in
the world, very rich eccentrics
take themselves to Basia
Zaryzka. Her exquisite hats are
smothered in silk and velvet
flowers, scraps of antique
fabrics, fascinating beads,
objets trouvés of all kinds; each
one is handmade and each is
unique – and they cost
anything from £95.00 to
£500.00. She also makes divine
decorated hatboxes (£199.00),
the only worthy receptacles for
such confections.
· · · ·
To go with the hats antique silk
shoes lavishly decorated with
beads and flowers (£450.00 a
pair, although you can have
your own decorated for
£165.00).
· · · ·
Ms Zaryzka champions the
preservation and recycling of
the beautiful; her shop
(Stand 3, Chenil Galleries,
181–183 King's Road, London
SW3 071 351 7276) is a
revelation.
· · · ·

Knitwear

MARION FOALE
13 Hinde Street
London W1
071 486 0239

Open: 10.00 to 6.00 Mon. to Fri;
10.00 to 5.00 Sat.
Credit Cards: Access, American
Express, Visa

Restrained classic knitwear in
unusual colours – subtle pastels
unfocussed greens etc. Much
natural fibre, and each piece comes
with full instructions on how to
care for it forever. Very expensive
(you won't get anything under
£100.00) but very beautiful.

Lingerie

COURTENAY
22 Brook Street
London W1
071 629 0542

Open: 10.00 to 6.00 Mon. to Fri;
late (7.00) Thurs; 10.00 to 5.00 Sat.
Credit Cards: Access, American
Express, Diners Club, Visa

Discreet, upmarket shop with a
glorious lingerie range (own label
Courtenay). Mouthwatering
delicate lace, satin and silk bras,
briefs, robes etc in silk, satin, fine
cotton. Small sizes (32 to 38). They
also sell elegant daywear and
accessories. Favourite with Royals,
elegant actresses (Patricia Hodge,
Diana Rigg). Expensive: lingerie
up to £700.00.

JANET REGER
2 Beauchamp Place
London SW3
071 584 9800

Open: 10.00 to 6.00 Mon. to Fri;
10.00 to 5.00 Sat.
Credit Cards: Access, American
Express, Diners Club, Visa

Rising indomitably from the ashes
of her previous empire, Janet Reger
is back selling her inimitable silky
undies. Expensive but irresistible.
Friendly, welcoming shop,
friendly staff; men love it in here.
David Owen, Prince Charles and
Barry Humphries(!) regular
customers.

Shoes

EMMA HOPE
33 Amwell Street
London EC1
071 833 2367

Open: 10.00 to 6.00 Mon. to Sat.
Credit Cards: Access, Visa

Gorgeous extravagant art-inspired
shoes: renaissance, baroque,
Vienna secessionist. Most of them
are not for everyday – lots of
embroidery, diverting heel shapes
and unusual materials. Collections
for Nicole Farhi, Betty Jackson and
others. Bridal shoes in abundance.
The shoes are displayed on a 'shoe
tree' (wirey branches spreading
over the shop.) Sizes are 2 to 9, and
prices are £69.00 to £130.00.

STEPHANE KELIAN
49a Sloane Street
London SW1
071 235 9098

Open: 10.00 to 5.30 Mon. to Sat;
late (7.00) Wed.

and
11 Grosvenor Street
London W1
071 355 3201

Open: 10.00 to 5.30 Mon. to Sat;
late (7.00) Thurs.
Credit Cards: Access, American
Express, Diners Club, Visa

Stephane Kelian shoes are
expensive (£90.00+) and
wonderful. Beautiful shapes, clever
texturing, glowing rich natural
colours: just go and look at them.
All are own label (sizes 2+ to 8) and
there are collections for Jean Paul
Gaultier and Claude Montana. Staff
are friendly and the Sloane Street
shop is tiny and welcoming. Tina
Turner buys her civvy shoes here.

JESSICA MOK
Studio 39
21 Clerkenwell Gardens
London EC1
071 251 2479

Open: 10.00 to 6.00 Mon. to Sat. by
appointment only

Not a shop but a working studio; a
selection of shoes on view from
which you can order, or special
one-offs made to match your
outfits. Sizes 3 to 8, very expensive
averaging £130.00.

SERIOUS UNDERWEAR
· · · ·
Rigby & Peller
2 Hans Road
Knightsbridge
London SW3
071 589 9293
· · · ·
Stately corset makers by
appointment to
H.R.H. The Queen.
Bounced back into the public
eye after *Madonna* introduced
the idea of wearing your undies
topside.
· · · ·
Made to measure boned satin
corsets here, and bras in every
conceivable size built by
experts: everything from
gossamer bandeaux to civil
engineering. Alterations done
on the premises.
· · · ·
Princess Margaret and
Marie Helvin keen customers.
· · · ·

SOUTH WEST LONDON

SW1

Knitwear

BEATRICE BELLINI HAND KNITS
74 Pimlico Road
London SW1W 8SL
071 730 2630

Open: 10.00 to 5.30 Mon. to Fri;
10.15 to 1.00 Sat.
Credit Cards: Access, American
Express, Visa

Beautiful made to measure hand
and machine knitted suits, dresses,
trousers, tops and jackets. Natural
fibres – shetland, mohair,
lambswool, silk and cotton.
Beatrice Bellini also makes up Kaffe
Fassett patterns and offers a unique
rescue service for the intrepid few
laypersons who embark on a
Fassett knitting pattern unaided,
and despair. (She will take your
effort away and knit it properly.)
Prices for Bellini designs range
from £75.00 for a jumper to
£250.00 to £300.00 for a knitted suit
that will last forever.

MOUSSIE
109 Walton Street
London SW3
071 581 8674

Open: 10.00 to 6.00 Mon. to Fri.
Credit Cards: Access, American
Express, Diners Club, Visa

Pretty pastel woodwork –
reminiscent of the delightful
domestic interiors by 19th century
Swedish architect Carl Larsson –
makes an appropriate settings for
delicious knitwear designed by
Moussie (herself Swedish).
Exclusive handknits in cotton wool
and cashmere: misty Fair Isles,
delicate lace trims, bright chunky
cotton knits. For the spring, little
suede skirts (brights and pastels) to
match; for the summer, a repeat of
last year's very successful shorts
and T shirts, hand stencilled to co-
ordinated with the knitwear. Sizes
10 to 14; expensive initial outlay
(£150.00 to £250.00), but not for
hand knit exclusivity: shorts and T
shirts at an affordable £40.00 to
£50.00. A refreshing change from
Latin knits.

Period & Antique Clothes

CORNUCOPIA
12 Tachbrook Street
London SW1
071 828 5752

Open: 10.00 to 6.00 Mon. to Sat.
Credit Cards: Access, American
Express, Visa

Small shop that lives up to its name:
you cannot see the walls (or indeed
ceiling) for the swags and swathes
of beautiful period costumes and
dresses, hats, shoes, bags, gloves,
arcane underwear and so on. Spend
hours in here, but not necessarily
many bucks: prices start at about
£10.00 and go upwards. Especially
good for wistful beaded tea gowns
and loads of gorgeous costume
jewellery. Sizes are of necessity
variable: there is reputed to be a
changing room at the back, but
don't go in without a guide.

Accessories

BACCARA
28 High Street
Wimbledon Village
London SW19
081 846 2298

Open: 10.00 to 5.30 Mon. to Sat.
Credit Cards: Access, American
Express, Diners Club, Visa

Shop for top seeded leather goods,
watches, scarves, gloves, costume
jewellery and bags. Names to be
thrown around the court are
Cartier, Yves Saint Laurent, Gucci,
Lanvin, Etienne Aigner. However,
price range covers £15.00 to
£1700.00. Two chairs to sit on
while you think about it. Very
good discreet service, great
attention to customers and
giftwrapping for items above a
fiver. Much used by tennis stars of
course, media folk and rock stars.
Another branch at David Lloyd
Slazenger Club, Bushey Road,
Raynes Park, London SW19.

Dress Hire

A CHANCE TO DANCE
57A Latchmere Road
London
SW11 2DS
071 350 1579

Open: 10.00 to 6.30 Mon. to Fri;
10.00 to 4.00 Sat.
Credit Cards: Access, American
Express, Visa

Ballgowns, cocktail dresses and
party frocks to hire, sizes 8 to 18; a
few designer labels, but most are
hand made original Chance to
Dance numbers. Hire fees are
£40.00 to £90.00 plus a £5.00
insurance (red wine does darken a
Dior) and a deposit of £150.00 (you
just give your credit card number).
Accessories also. All the dresses are
for sale, and you can have an
original made for you.

20th CENTURY FROX
827 Fulham Road
London SW6 5HG
071 731 3242

Open: 10.00 to 7.00 Mon. to Fri;
10.00 to 5.00 Sat.
Credit Cards: Access, American
Express, Diners Club, Visa

Designer Frock Hire. All labels, all
styles in sizes 8 to 18. Expect to pay
between £40.00 and £90.00. Also
co-ordinating costume jewellery.

Hats

JANE SMITH STRAW HATS
131 St Philip Street
London SW8 3SS
071 627 2414

Open: 10.00 to 6.00 Mon. to Fri;
10.00 to 5.00 Sat.
Credit Cards: Access, Visa

Beautifully made hats, straw and
otherwise. Uncluttered,
professional shop that concentrates
on their unique product (if you look
in the window, you will want all of
them). The designers work on the
premises in the studio upstairs, so
are on hand to advise and help
customers. The staff are very
friendly and helpful, the hats are
just plain gorgeous (they range
from £75.00 to £300.00 and are
worth every centime). All sizes;
alterations and a refurbishment
service available; they will also build
you a hat to order. Hat boxes in
three sizes on sale. They make loads
of period titfers for films and TV.

Lingerie

TEMPTATIONS
64 High Street
Wimbledon Village
London SW19
081 946 5624

Open: 9.30 to 5.30 Mon. to Sat.
Credit Cards: Access, American
Express, Visa

Run by lingerie buyers who
jumped ship from M & S. Bra
fitting a speciality. La Perla,
Malizia, Lejaby, Patricia, Gossard;
(sizes 32 upwards, a to e cups); wide
variety of nightwear (small to extra
large); swimwear from La Perla,
Gideon Oberson and a new range
from Robbie Cranfield – part of the
Ken Done Oz team, but rather
more sophisticated designs.
Friendly, discreet, knowledgeable
staff. They will also help plan bridal
trousseaux. Temptations also in
WEYBRIDGE.

Special Sizes

BASE
Rushka Murganovic
273 New King's Road
London SW6
071 736 8061

Open: 10.00 to 6.00 Mon. to Sat;
late (7.00) Thurs.
Credit Cards: Access, American
Express, Diners Club, Visa

A second shop full of great clothes
for sizes 14 to 28. For details see
page 102.

SOUTH EAST

Lingerie

SHE
32 Tranquil Vale
London SE3
081 852 5310

Open: 9.30 to 5.30 Mon. to Sat.
Credit Cards: Access, American
Express, Diners Club, Visa

Very traditional, well-established
shop – all original mahogany
fittings; dove coloured carpet and
pink drapes give an intimate
homely atmosphere. Impressive
range of upmarket lingerie – La
Perla, Malizia, Lejaby, Lisa
Charmel, Robin Alexis. Excellent
bra size range from aa through to f;
alterations available free.
Swimwear from La Perla, Gideon
Oberson, Rassurelle, Gottex (sizes
10 to 18). Good range of nightwear
(sizes small to extra large). Very
good sales in January and August;
silk undies at Christmas. Selective
range of scent (for men and
women). The window display is
award winning: it changes weekly.

RICHMOND, BARNES & TWICKENHAM

YVONNE DAMANT
2 The Square
Richmond TW9 1DY
081 940 0514

Open: 10.00 to 6.00 Mon. to Sat.
Credit Cards: Access, Visa

GREENWICH MARKET
····
Greenwich High Road
London SE10
····
All day Sundays
····
Get there early for the best
bargains; antique and second
hand clothes to be found at the
rear of the open air section of
the Antique Market: shoes,
hats, accessories. Be prepared
to sift through piles of jumble
in search of a bargain: treasures
from 30s, 40s, 50s and 60s to be
scored by the hawklike of eye.
····

Delightfully unusual and
idiosyncratic shop, with stone urns
and decorative iron work by local
blacksmith. Definitely the place to
go if you like unique, well made
and interesting clothes. Relaxed
atmosphere, browse as you will
without pressure. Clothes are
displayed hanging up on the walls.
Very individual choice of
designers: Sybilla, Dolce and
Gabbana, Galliano, Fujiwara and
Ozbek; Gabriela Ligenza hats,
Dinny Hall jewellery. Most people
go for Yvonne's own label clothes,
which are based on period designs:
currently 1910 fashions; ready to
wear and made to order. Sizes are 8
to 16, prices range from £40.00 to
£600.00. All sorts of people shop
here: art students save up for an
ensemble, business women buy
several at a time. Clothes with
personality.

HELEN HAYES
70 Church Road
Barnes
London SW13
081 741 0456

Open: 10.00 to 6.00 Mon. to Sat.
Credit Cards: Access, American
Express, Visa; Helen Hayes
account

Bright, light and spacious with
spiffing great mirrors; pleasing
atmosphere, good for envious
browsing. Luscious clothes:
Ventilo, John Galliano, Edina
Ronay, Montana, Margaret
Howell, Workers for Freedom,
Katherine Hamnett, Ralph Lauren,
Ally Cappellino. Sizes 8 to 14,
alterations available; private
changing rooms. Shoes from
Robert Clergerie and Stephane
Kelian (drool, drool); jewellery
from Dinny Hall. There is no
reason for Barnes stylies to fight
their way through the west end of
London (the noise! the people!)
when they have all this and personal
friendly service on their doorsteps.
Prices range from acceptable to
very expensive.

HOURGLASS
5 Sheen Road
Richmond
081 332 0166

Open: 10.00 to 6.00 Mon. to Fri;
9.30 to 6.00 Sat.
Credit Cards: Access, Transax, Visa

Slick black and chrome boîte selling
designer party and cocktail frocks
and separates. Most clothes from
Sara Whitworth, and they move so
fast and the designs are so
individual you are unlikely to see
the same thing twice. Only for
those in good shape: sizes are 8/10
and 12/14 (alterations available).
You can buy a bustier for £32.00;
dresses up to £450.00. Made to
measure one-offs also available.
Friendly, helpful staff; a second
branch (called Deadlier than the
Male) in Hyper Hyper
(see page 109).

JULES
74 Tower Road
Strawberry Hill
Twickenham
081 892 8776

Open: 9.00 to 5.30 Mon. to Sat; late
(7.00) on Thurs.
Credit Cards: Access, Barclaycard

Small, welcoming shop with
gorgeous unusual windows; it's
owned and run by two ex-models
so they know what they are doing.
Carefully chosen range of
continental daywear, (Hucke,
Ponzi, Jerry Webber); casual
cottons from Stephanie; lingerie
from Lejaby. A real effort is made
to restrict the number of items
ordered in any one range, so that
each customer (and they have a
strong local following) develops an
individual look. Sizes are 8 to 20
and alterations are carried out free.
Very personal caring service.

VIEW
17 Hill Street
Richmond TW9 15X
081 332 2726

Open: 10.00 to 6.00 Mon. to Sat.
Credit Cards: Access, American
Express, Diners Club, Visa

Branch of the very smart shop for
men and women in HAMPSTEAD.
High profile design labels, helpful
informed staff. For confident
achievers who understand good
design when they see it.

....

WORKSHOP
224 Upper Richmond Road
East Sheen
London SW14
081 878 6979

Open: 10.00 to 6.00 Mon. to Sat.
Credit Cards: Access, American
Express, Transax, Visa

Relaxed, unhassled shop in the
Mulberry mode – mellow pine,
Persian rugs; relaxed, effortless chic
to match: clothes from Betty
Jackson, Edina Ronay, Arabella
Pollen, Paul Costelloe Dressage,
Synonyme, KL, English
Eccentrics; Arabel Fox knitwear;
Osprey belts; shoes from Fratelli
Rossetti, Robert Clergerie, Joseph
Azaguri. Mulberry accessories.
Prices from £50.00 to £200.00.
Each collection nonchalantly
gathered in separate area; private
changing rooms. Sizes 8 to 16,
alterations available. Media persons
and celeb wives shop here.
Branch in Chiswick soon.

....

Bags & Accessories

TANNERS
8 Hill Street
Richmond TW9 1TN
081 332 1655

Open: 9.30 to 6.00 Mon. to Sat.
Credit Cards: Access, American
Express, Diners Club, Visa

Splendid shop for bags, shoes and
accessories. Warm gleaming wood
fittings and very friendly helpful
staff. Own label leather bags,
briefcases, overnight bags, wallets,
writing cases in a wide variety of
styles (prices from £45.00 to
£150.00); also Mulberry . Lovely
own label loafers and lace-ups in
plaited leather and plain (sizes 35 to
41). Jewellery and scarves from
Wright and Teague; Fred Bare hats.
Paul Smith socks, ties and scarves
for the chaps. There are also
Tanners in CHISWICK and
HAMPSTEAD.

....

TANNERS
2 Turnham Green Terrace
Chiswick
London W4 1QP
081 994 4762

Open: 9.30 to 6.00 Mon. to Sat.
Credit Cards: Access, American
Express, Diners Club, Visa

Splendid friendly shop selling own
label all leather bags and shoes, jolly
Fred Bare hats and stylish
jewellery. See RICHMOND.

....

THE SOUTH

· · · · · · · · · ·

HAMPSHIRE, KENT, SUSSEX

Most fashion shoppers in the South
depend on London or are sucked into the
mega high streets of Croydon or
Guildford. Some pockets of initiative
left: go to Southampton for young
enterprise; Lymington for blue-chip
Jaeger; and Brighton for almost
everything, from high octane designer
chic via recycled americana to elegant
antique tea gowns.

HAMPSHIRE

SOUTHAMPTON

ANGEL GABRIEL
31 Northam Road
Southampton SO2 0NZ
0703 332380

Open: 10.00 to 5.00 Mon. to Sat.
Credit Cards: Access, American
Express, Diners Club, Visa

Brand new shop for the designs of
Angela Barter and Gabrielle
Hookings; ready to wear and made
to measure clothes (the workshop is
at the back). For their first summer
they are doing a white collection –
simple unstructured shapes, elastic
waists (joy), lots of one-size stuff.
Rather good party wear – much
lycra and stretchy glitz. They have
a portfolio of designs to browse
through and photographs of their
clothes in action on the wall. Prices
are good: £20.00 to £200.00.

LYMINGTON

JAEGER AT JOSEPHINE WARREN
116 High Street
Lymington
0590 678259

Open: 9.00 to 5.30 Mon. to Sat.
Credit Cards: Access, American
Express, Diners Club, Visa

Classic, timeless elegant dressing
here. One of the very few
independent Jaeger stockists; sells
only Jaeger clothes, carrying the
whole range from Cameo (for the
5.0 to 5.2″ woman) upwards to size
20. Once yearly collection of
evening wear (October); classic
daywear, expanding now into the
more casual weekend range.
Wonderful, friendly informed
service from the owners who know
their Jaeger inside out; coffee served
while you buy. Gorgeous black
moiré silk settee where husbands
can recline sipping sherry while the
serious clothes buying goes on.

Shoes

COPPELIA
8 St Thomas Street
Lymington SO4 9NA
0590 676370

Open: 9.30 to 5.30 Mon. to Sat.
Credit Cards: Access, American
Express, Diners Club, Visa

Former shoe shop that's gradually
transforming itself into an all
purpose clothes purveyor to the
casual chic. Sara Sturgeon
Clothing, MaxMara, Betty
Jackson, Muir & Osborne
knitwear, Etienne Aigner, Jean
Muir Studio, Mulberry accessories.
Swimwear by Oceana. Shoes are all
Italian, and mainly in the elegant
pump and street line to go with the
clothes. Sizes 2 upwards. Lovely
old shop with elusive nautical
atmosphere (lots of wooden beams
and a spiral staircase); most
customers come from London
though: Lymington yotties only
ever wear rubber boots.

KENT

HOOPERS LIMITED
The Great Hall
Mount Pleasant Road
Tunbridge Wells TN1 1QQ
0892 510530

Open: 9.15 to 5.30 Mon. to Sat.
Credit Cards: Access, American
Express, Diners Club, Visa;
Hoopers Account Card

One of the Hoopers chain of
fashion oriented department stores.
Excellent range of Eurolabels,
good accessories, 16+ department.
There are also Hoopers in
CHELTENHAM, CHICHESTER,
COLCHESTER, TORQUAY,
WILMSLOW. See also Dukes in
EXETER.

Special Sizes

OPINIONS
7 Palace Street
Canterbury
0227 472649

Open: 9.30 to 5.30 Mon. to Sat.
Credit Cards: Access, American
Express, Visa

Another branch of the splendid
Opinions shops; the same range as
the main shop in BRIGHTON, plus
lingerie to fit sizes 16 to 30.
Another Opinions in GUILDFORD.

SUSSEX

BRIGHTON

ANANDA
38 Kensington Gardens
Brighton
0273 697096

Open: 9.30 to 5.30 Mon. to Sat.
Credit Cards: Access, American
Express, Diners Club, Visa

Ethnic hippy clothes grow up;
excellent shop for own design
stylish drapey jackets, wide
cropped pants, topsé skirts and
unstructured dresses which can be
mixed and matched. Hand blocked
prints in formal colours; good
enough for party wear for those
frightened of dressing up. Loose
cut means generous sizing – 10 to
16(ish). Prices to match: jackets
around £40.00. Good selection of
unusual 'barbarian' jewellery to
team with it; also floaty scarves and
squashy hats.

THE CLASSIC CLOTHING
COMPANY
39 Gardner Street
Brighton
0273 695851

Open: 10.00 to 6.00 Mon. to Sat.
Credit Cards: Access, American
Express, Visa

Small, relaxed shop for the young
and smart: sell Neoline (from the
designers who jumped ship at

Whistles), Soap Studio, WilliWear and Betty Jackson. Sizes 10 to 14, prices £15.00 to £150.00. Look for the distinctive dada logo – huge CCC in rusty iron across the window.

FORM
56 Western Road
Brighton
0273 734536

Open: 9.30 to 6.00 Mon. to Sat; late (7.00) Thurs.
Credit Cards: Access, American Express, Mastercard, Visa

Oasis of style among the multiples and jeaneries of Brighton's main shopping street. Spacious shop with a strong sense of identity; large range of separates from Pamplemousse and Pamplemousse Collection; smart casual suits from Wash House; Pink Soda T shirts; saucy party numbers from Sugar. All in sizes 8 to 14. Interesting shoe collection (Italian own label) displayed among the clothes; off-beat arty-stylish designs. Prices are good: clothes £20.00 to £80.00(ish); shoes around £30.00 to £50.00. Upstairs for chaps' clothes. Two other Forms: South Molton and Oxford Streets, London.

LIBERTY's
East Street
Brighton
0273 822933

Open: 9.30 to 6.00 Mon. to Sat; late (6.30) Thurs.
Credit Cards: Access, American Express, Diners Club, Visa

STREET SMART
• • • •
Although **The Lanes** is probably the bit of Brighton most visitors know best, the place for young street fashion is
North Laines
to the east of the main street.
• • • •
Aim for Gardner Street, Kensington Gardens and Sidney Street for unusual street chic. Fashion forces dictate that shops in this patch change hands fairly rapidly, but it's the place to spot up and coming talent and new ideas.
Here you can find
ROKIT
(23 Kensington Gardens) one of the small chain that sell good quality second hand clothes recycled from America – mostly Levis, Hawaiian shirts, the occasional Top Gun flying jacket – great for authentic retro dressing.
• • • •
Every Saturday morning there is an unpredictable junk market in
Upper Gardner Street.
• • • •

A small outpost of olde world art nouveau charm: a microcosm of the mother ship carrying a compact selection of Liberty's own label clothes (men and women). Strong on accessories: scarves, hair bands.

LE MAGASIN
12 Market Street,
The Lanes
Brighton
0273 23762

Open: 9.30 to 5.30 Mon. to Sat.
Credit Cards: Access, American
Express, Diners Club, Visa

V. elegant glamorous shop with a
small range of ultra high chic
(Alaia, Myrène de Prémonville) for
the young rich. Dinny Hall
jewellery. Sizes 8 to 14, prices start
at £80.00 for a blouse and after that
the only way is up. Sales at New
Year. Rather intimidating
atmosphere is humanised by a
resident (and permanently snoring)
golden cocker spaniel called
Gabriella.

NAMES
6 Dukes Lane
Brighton
0273 28807

Open: 10.00 to 6.00 Mon. to Sat.
Credit Cards: Access, American
Express, Diners Club, Visa

Sagacious owner Frances Conway
buys weekly, direct from London
wholesalers or overstocked top
shops. This allows her to sell
Lauren, Armani, Versace, Oldfield
etc for less than half their usual price
(expect to pay £30.00 to £450.00).
Mostly women's clothes (sizes 8 to
16), alterations possible – coats,
separates, serious suits, strong
evening wear section; also hats,
bags and sometimes shoes.

NATALY
7 Bartholomews Square
Brighton BN1 1GS
0273 202915

Open: 10.00 to 6.00 Mon. to Sat.
Credit Cards: Access, American
Express, Visa

Chic little boutique on Brighton's
newest Square with helpful, well
informed owner; they sell
upmarket, wearable clothes for
20+ women: Paul Costelloe,
Zucchero, Italian labels. Quite
pricey (up to £400.00) but very
agreeable. Sizes 10 to 14.

SALUTE
6 Gardner Street
Brighton
0273 606459

Open: 10.00 to 6.00 Mon. to Sat.
Credit Cards: Access, American
Express, Visa

Fearsomely chic shop with
distressed plaster walls and hi tech
changing rooms that look like a
couple of alien cheesegraters.
However, staff surprisingly helpful
and friendly; they sell high fashion
streetwear for the up to 35s,
featuring Simple Standards,
Waterland Affairs; Galliano T-
shirts; Fenn, Wright & Manson
separates and Aviatic jeans. Rather
good silk shirts and blouses from
their own label (Salute); knitwear
by Walter and local designer Mary
Rene. Sizes 10 to 14; expect to
spend anything from £45.00 to
£200.00 (for a suit).

SAXS
2 Union Street
Brighton
0273 24646

Open: 9.30 to 6.00 Mon. to Sat.
Credit Cards: Access, American
Express, Diners Club, Visa

Shop for the younger set in the
minimal chic mode. Women's
clothes in the basement: wackier
styles and slightly cheaper than
grown-up Saxs (see below): Sara
Sturgeon, Katherine Hamnett,
Betty Jackson, Ben de Lisi, Junior
Gaultier. Sizes 10 to 16. Excellent
sales (January and June).

There is another Saxs in
GLASGOW.

....

SAXS
3 Bartholomews
Brighton
0273 21654

Open: 9.00 to 6.00 Mon. to Sat. and
by appointment
Credit Cards: Access, American
Express, Diners Club, Visa

The kind of blissful establishment
outside which the stylish but
temporarily financially
embarrassed wistfully lurk. Two
floors: seductive restrained luxury
downstairs; more opulence
upstairs, to go with the more
expensive clothes. The staff are
friendly and helpful, the regular
clientele go there for classic,
elegant, grown up clothes: Genny
and Versace, Romeo Gigli, Ozbek,
Gianfranco Ferre, Moschino,
Norma Kamali, Montana.

Ginochietti etc etc. Anita Roddick
(Body Shop began in Brighton)
shops here. Sizes range from 10 to
16, and prices begin at £50.00 and
go up. A six-month free credit
scheme allows regulars to stock up
at the beginning of the season.
There's also a February catalogue
(phone for one). There is a smaller
Saxs a few minutes walk away in
Union Street (see above) and
another in GLASGOW.

....

21 DUKES LANE
21 Duke's Lane
Brighton
0273 206058

Open: 10.00 to 6.00 Mon. to Sat.
Credit Cards: Access, American
Express, Diners Club, Visa

Large(ish) shop in Brighton's
famous Lanes. Owner/designer
Deborah Kessel sells a very
wearable range of separates in
natural fibres: wool jersey, linen,
raw silk, cotton and cotton jersey.
Good colours and relaxed unfussy
styles in sizes 10 to 16. Prices start
at £25.00 and a raw silk suit will
cost about £300.00. The design
workshop is behind the shop and
they will make up their styles in
extra small or large sizes, different
lengths or colours on request. Nice
range of hats and belts and English
Eccentrics silk range. Strong local
following of stylish 30+ women
who like individual clothes.

....

Hats

HATTERS
69 Western Road
Hove BN3 1JB
0273 25933

Open: 9.45 to 5.30 Mon. to Sat.
Credit Cards: Access, American
Express, Visa

Smallish shop in plum and pink
with mahogany display cabinets;
very full of hats, all carrying their
own label. Good range of stylish
workaday hats – felts, velvet berets,
straws in summer etc as well as
frivolous cocktail numeros. Special
occasion hats feature strongly, and
they will make up an elaborate hair
comb for those who still can't face a
proper hat. Prices from £15.00 to
£200.00, £12.00 to £40.00 for the
haircombs. Trilbies, caps and
panamas for men (and girls with
heroic head measurements).
Interesting selection of hatpins,
including Victorian ones, and hat
boxes.

Jewellery

CLIVE & PHILIP
66 St James Street
Brighton BN2 1PJ
0273 676833

Open: 10.00 to 5.30 Mon. to Sat.
Credit Cards: Access, Visa

Next door to the divine WARDROBE
(see page 128) this is the antique
shop run by Clive Parks and Philip
Parfitt. A tiny shop with inspired
window displays, lovingly
crammed with antique and period
objets d'art, china, glass,
stationery, accessories of
yesteryear. You can stay in here for
hours and not see everything.
Wonderful range of authentic
period costume jewellery,
Edwardian onwards, including
smashing crystal and diamanté
necklaces and earrings from the
1950s. Stock is snapped up
regularly by the discerning and so
changes all the time. Clive and
Philip are so helpful you want to
cry.

RUBY JONES
33 Duke Street
Brighton
0273 202354

Open: 10.00 to 6.00 Mon. to Sat.
Credit Cards: Access, American
Express, Diners Club, Visa

Not for the sensible or retiring,
Ruby Jones is a magnificently
uninhibited establishment with a
wonderful collection of huge glitzy
earrings and unique costume
jewellery that cannot fail to lift the
spirit. To go with the jools, an
inspired collection of unashamedly
glam and often OTT party clothes
and separates (sizes 10 to 16) to
dress your dearest Bette Midler
fantasies. The house scent
(Reminisce) is equally heady.
Below stairs you can cop a sun tan
in the sunbed parlour; upstairs they
sell Raybans for when the real thing
is doing its stuff.

INSIDE OUT
34a–36 Upper St James Street
Brighton
0273 674819

Open: 10.00 to 6.00 Mon. to Sat.
Credit Cards: Access, American
Express, Visa

Unlikely shop at first glance, as it
concentrates on home decoration
(mirrors, wooden furniture,
stencilling materials etc) but inside
it has a wide selection of unusual
and not very expensive silver
earrings, brooches and necklaces.
Also covetable filigree silver
perfume bottles. Collier Campbell
scarves and shawls and excellent
stout leather briefcase-style bags.
Charming shop with very helpful
owners who are always there.

....

TUCAN
29 Bond Street
Brighton BN1 1RD
0273 26531

Open: 10.00 to 5.00 Mon. to Sat.
Credit Cards: Access, Mastercard,
Visa

Large shop that does its best to
convince you that you are indeed in
the Andes (straw ceiling, pan pipes
music, flocks of gorgeous balsa
wood parrots and toucans.) An
excellent hunting ground for
inexpensive Mexican silver and
turquoise jewellery – earrings,
rings, necklaces – for the ethnic
look. Also at the back of the shop,
rough colourful all-cotton shirts,
ponchos, straw hats and those
tough felt Peruvian bowlers to
build up a convincing gaucho look
at a fraction of the price charged by
high profile designers. No
changing rooms, but beautiful
hand carved and decorated mirrors
(which are for sale). Helpful
informed staff, and lots of jolly bits
and pieces to look at.

....

Knitwear

CLOTHES RAIL
16 Gardner Street
Brighton
0273 689011

Open: 10.00 to 6.00 Mon. to Sat.
Credit Cards: Access, Visa

Carolyn Sadler's delicious knits:
small range of classic skirts, tops,
dresses, jumpers in wonderful
colours and natural fibres. Sizes s,
m and l; all own label (Clothes
Rail). If you like Marion Foale, then
you can buy beautiful clothes in the
same vein here for a fraction of the
price (£10.00 to £50.00). Also a
range of eccentric and delectable
hats (£20.00 to £50.00), probably
only for the young and brave.

....

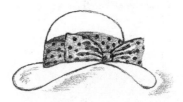

Lingerie

MARY GRAEME
3–4 Regent Arcade
East Street
Brighton BN1 1HR
0273 25255

Open: 10.00 to 5.30 Mon. to Sat.
Credit Cards: Access, American
Express, Diners Club, Visa

Lovely relaxed shop which sells
shoes, lingerie and a small range of
clothes. See SHOES (below) for
more details.

Made to Order

THE DESIGN STUDIO
19 George Street
Brighton BN2 1RH
0273 681369

Open: 11.00 to 6.00 or 7.00 Mon. to
Sat.
Credit Cards: None

Very small shop run by designer
Patricia Durrant. What you see in
the shop are samples of Durrant's
range of simple classic designs in
natural fabrics: silk, cotton, viyella,
pure wool. When you have made
your choice, she will make it up in
your size and the colours you like.
You can supply your own material
if you like. It takes about a week
and prices start at £20.00,
depending on size, elaboration etc.
Excellent place to find well priced
individual clothes for the 25 ups.

Period & Antique Clothes

LEOPARD
35 Kensington Gardens
Brighton
0273 695427

Open: 10.30 to 4.00 Mon. to Fri;
10.30 to 5.00 Sat.
Credit Cards: Access, American
Express, Diners Club, Visa

Largish cave-like shop hung
about with lots of good quality
antique white linen and lace
nighties, shirts, tablecloths; also
dashing brocade and velvet
waistcoats and Byronic fencing
shirts. Sizes are approximate, as
with most antique clothes.

WARDROBE
68 St James Street
Brighton
0273 676833

Open: 10.00 to 5.30 Mon. to Sat.
Credit Cards: Access, Visa

Absolutely gorgeous shop with
swoon-making window display.
Period clothes for men and women;
nothing after the 1940s. It is owned
by Clive Parks and Philip Parfitt (of
CLIVE & PHILIP next door) and run
by them and one lady helper. A tiny
shop, full of immaculate clothes
that exude lost glamour. Prices are
£25.00 upwards (expect to pay
about £200.00 for a beaded evening
gown) and they have to be tried on
for fit. Hats from £12.00 to £60.00
and period costume jewellery to
match. Gentle thé dansant music

reinforces the ambience of civilized elegance; Wardrobe are often called upon by TV producers kitting out period drama pieces and is much loved and patronized by Brighton's theatrical set (Simon Fanshawe, Steven Berkoff) as well as art students, fashion journos and anyone who likes to dress with originality and flair.

....

Shoes

MARY GRAEME
3–4 Regent Arcade
East Street
Brighton BN1 1HR
0273 25255

Open: 10.00 to 5.30 Mon. to Sat.
Credit Cards: Access, American Express, Diners Club, Visa

Warm friendly relaxed shop with loyal clientele, including theatricals. It sprawls gently over two shop areas with a mezzanine. Difficult to categorise, as the specialities are shoes and lingerie. Shoes (all B fitting) from sizes 3 to 8: imaginative range from various continental designers and well edited boot selection. Lingerie rather glam – Lejaby, Louis Feraud, La Perla – prices from £25.00 to £140.00. Chaps flock here at Christmas time. Scrummy pure silk and pure cotton nighties and robes in a wide size range. Six deliveries per season ensures an ever changing stock. Two private changing rooms to try them on in. A mail order catalogue is available every September. Swimwear by

Ken Done.

They also sell a small range of easy to wear casual clothes (sizes 10 to 16) at modest prices (£50.00/£60.00) – what Sarah Hinton (Mrs Graeme) calls 'housekeeping' clothes, because you can wangle them out of your monthly budget.

....

Special Sizes

OPINIONS
16 Church Street
Brighton
0273 27240

Open: 9.30 to 5.30 Mon. to Sat.
Credit Cards: Access, American Express, Visa

Terrific shop for career women of exuberant shape. Streamlined black and white decor and a saucy new logo of unashamed Rubens nude. Very smart clothes from Hesselhoj, Big is Beautiful, Steel and Reeves, Givenchy 42 to 52 and own label Original Opinions in sizes 16 to 30. Excellent ranges of dressy evening separates. T-shirts, belts, tights and jewellery as well. Prices start at £20.00 for a T-shirt and go up to £400.00 to £500.00. Large changing room, coffee offered while you ponder, and knowledgeable, friendly, unspindly staff. Every August 14th they have a birthday party and preview new collections. There is a mail order service (send a large SAE), but sadly they have discontinued their party frock hire.

Other Opinions in CANTERBURY and GUILDFORD.

....

CHICHESTER

HOOPERS LIMITED
St Peter's House
North Street
Chichester PO19 1LT
0243 533103

Open: 9.15 to 5.30 Mon. to Sat.
Credit Cards: Access, American
Express, Diners Club, Visa

One of the Hoopers chain of
fashion oriented department stores.
Excellent range of eurolabels, good
accessories, 16+ department.
There are also Hoopers in
CHELTENHAM, COLCHESTER,
TORQUAY, TUNBRIDGE WELLS,
WILMSLOW. See also DUKES in
EXETER.

CUCKFIELD

BLOSSOMS
High Street
Cuckfield RH17 5SX
0444 459978

Open: 9.30 to 5.30 Mon. to Sat.
Credit Cards: Access, American
Express, Diners Club, Visa

Small chic establishment selling
high class labels and accessories in
this pretty country town. Roland
Klein, KL, Ginochietti, Gaston
Jaunet, Bellville Sassoon, Laurel,
L'Estelle; Viv Knowland hats,
jewellery from Butler & Wilson,
Christian Dior. Sizes 8 to 16,
alterations available. Next door is
their shoe shop, selling KL,
Jourdan and Luc Berjen.

LEWES

CAPRICCIO
163 High Street
Lewes
0273 474354

Open: 9.30 to 5.30 Mon. to Sat;
closes at 1.30 on Wed.
Credit Cards: Access, Visa

Delightful small(ish) shop with
exposed beams for rural chic.
Helpful friendly staff – particularly
tactful with blundering husbands
apparently. Good for relaxed, easy
to wear clothes with an elegant
ethnic dimension – Adini, Anokhi,
Monsoon. Lots of natural fabrics.
Nice selection of French
Connection, Fenn, Wright &
Manson, and rather good shirts
from The Shirtmaker. Small
selection of partywear. Sizes 10 to
16, although the style of some of
the clothes will accommodate a
16+. Four private changing rooms.
Hats from Bermona and Viv
Knowland; Osprey belts; Java
jewellery and jolly kelim bags.
Prices range from £10.00 to
£150.00.

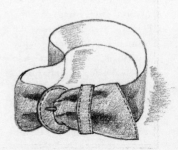

SCOTLAND

· · · · · · · · · ·

Very high level fashion in Scotland:
people dress more formally here, and it
shows: go to Aberdeen for exciting
young Dutch (yes Dutch) labels;
Auchterarder for impeccable tweeds and
cashmeres; Edinburgh for prime
dressing; and of course Glasgow for
totally terminal chic.

ABERDEEN

GOING DUTCH
7 Rosemount Viaduct
Aberdeen
0224 624221

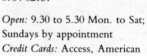

Open: 10.30 to 6.00 Mon. to Sat.
Credit Cards: Access, Visa

Outpost of Netherland chic in Scotland: great designer clothes with interesting inventive touches, seaming details and good shapes. Twisted Sister, Soap Studio, Nieuw Amsterdam Peil; as a concession to 1992 there is a small range of Italian and French wear. Some men's clothes and hats. Sizes 10 to 16, prices reasonable. Also great new pendant jewellery by Prior Maclean. Great sale in January/February. Echt Hollands owner.

RAGS
29 Rose Street
Aberdeen
0224 643264

Open: 9.30 to 5.30 Mon. to Thurs; 9.30 to 5.00 Fri. and Sat.
Credit Cards: Access, American Express, Diners Club, Visa

Sophisticated elegant shop (cream watered silk and gold decor) for 25+ fashionables. Good range of wearable mid price to expensive labels: Monsoon, Marc Cain, JH Collectibles, Susan Croft, Nicole Farhi, Arabella Pollen, KL; knitwear from Edina Ronay and Soft Options. Also posh suits and designer ballgowns. Sizes 8 to 16 and they will organize alterations. Private changing rooms, coffee on offer. There is another Rags in BRECHIN.

AUCHTERARDER

R. WATSON HOGG
50 Main Street
Auchterarder
Perthshire
0764 62151

Open: 9.30 to 5.30 Mon. to Sat; Sundays by appointment
Credit Cards: Access, American Express, Diners Club, Visa

Splendid two floor olde worlde establishment bristling with stuffed beasts of the glen and mahogany presses. The largest range of Ballantyne knitwear in the known world; also cashmere from N.Peal (who bought the shop last year). You can have a tweed suit built here; bolts and bolts of sartorially impeccable cloth to choose from. Well chosen range of beautiful classic skirts, dresses and separates, cashmere coats, travelling rugs, scarves and shawls. Gleneagles is but one mile away, and golfing togs abound – sensible polo tops, very silly trousers, giant tartan umbrellas. Also sell Barbour and other working country wear. Eat your heart out Richard Hannay.

BRECHIN

RAGS
23 Clark Street
Brechin
03562 5313

Open: 9.30 to 5.30 Mon. to Sat.
Credit Cards: Access, American
Express, Diners Club, Visa

Second shop to Rags in ABERDEEN
carrying a similar range of elegant,
wearable clothes from impeccable
labels: Nicole Farhi, KL, Arabella
Pollen etc. Sizes 8 to 16, prices
affordable to expensive.

EDINBURGH

CAMPUS
42 Grassmarket
Edinburgh
031 226 5564

Open: 9.30 to 5.30 Mon. to Fri; 9.00
to 6.00 Sat.
Credit Cards: Access, American
Express, Diners Club, Visa

Intelligent fashion for the 20+: KL,
Jean Muir and Jean Muir Studio,
Ginochietti, Terence Nolder etc.
Belts and scarves, Jean Muir
jewellery. Slightly cheaper, and
very individual is their own
Academy Collection label,
designed by Betty Davis, owner of
the Campuses. The Academy
Collection covers separates, suits,
evening wear, wild coloured Harris
tweed, silk ballgowns, classic
daywear and some jersey. Also
Academy hats – eccentric
Bloomsbury(ish) headgear for

**THE HARRODS O' THE
NORTH**
····
This title sits easily on the
magnificent Jenners,
in Princes Street Edinburgh.
····
It's a Rolls Royce of a store:
chauffeurs still drive up to pick
up the parcels, and it has
everything an Edinburgh lady
could want.
····

---

brainy romantics. Sizes 8 to 16,
prices affordable to expensive; six
month charge account available.

There are Campuses in GLASGOW
and OXFORD; the Acadamy
Collection *tout seul* can be found in
the Betty Davis Academy at 39
Hanover Street, Edinburgh.

CRUISE
14 St Mary's Street
Edinburgh
031 556 2532

Open: 10.00 to 6.00 Mon. to Fri;
9.30 to 6.00 Sat.
Credit Cards: Access, American
Express, Diners Club, Visa

A branch of the GLASGOW shop
selling affordable young street
casuals to the young and spindly.
Soap Studio, Mathilde, Nicola
Georgiou, denims, leather. Sizes 8
to 12. Chaps' clothes here too.

CORNICHE
2 Jeffrey Street
Edinburgh EH1 1DT
031 556 3707

Open: 10.00 to 5.30 Mon. to Sat.
Credit Cards: Access, American
Express, Diners Club, Visa

Largish relaxed well stocked shop
for design minded grown ups (20
upwards). Excellent labels: Betty
Jackson, Sara Sturgeon, Nicole
Farhi, Ghost, Transit, Twisted
Sister, Prémonville Studio, John
Rochas, Hamnett II, Ami Modo
knitwear. Sizes 10 to 14;
alterations. Small range of
menswear.

THE DESIGNER SHOP
49 William Street
Edinburgh
031 225 3756

Open: 10.00 to 5.30 Mon. to Sat.
Credit Cards: Access, Visa

Clothes for smart brisk girls to
grow up in: north euro chic
(Barouche, Signature, Jerry
Webber, Meyer Mode) and a lone
Brit, Husen (nice velvet shorty
jackets and culottes) Good
inexpensive range of separates from
Lebek (£20.00 plus).

DROOPY & BROWNS
37 to 39 Frederick Street
Edinburgh
031 225 1019

Open: 10.00 to 6.00 Mon. to Fri;
9.30 to 5.30 Sat.
Credit Cards: Access, Visa

Own label day and evening wear;
the same stock as in YORK. Droopy
& Browns are also in BATH and
LONDON.

ANDREA MACKIE
45 William Street
Edinburgh
031 220 0320

Open: 10.00 to 5.00 Mon. to Fri.
Credit Cards: Access, Visa

Well-established shop selling
wearable classics for stylish
professional women: Caroline
Charles, Guy Laroche, Ports, Paul
Costelloe, Susan Crofts, Stephen
Brothers; scarves and gloves from
Cornelia James. Good news for the
tiny: sizes range from 6 to 16. They
have their own label, Andrea
Mackie, classic sweaters and shirts
at a very reasonable £30.00 or so.
Relaxed and helpful staff in a small
informal shop. Very hot on
personal service (for instance they
will order up nonstock colours or
design a one-off to your
specifications). They are moving to
a bigger shop in Stafford Street in
the summer; the fate of the William
Street shop hangs in the balance.

SWING
60 Grassmarket
Edinburgh
031 226 7046

Open: 10.00 to 6.00 Mon. to Sat.
Credit Cards: Access, Visa

Small shop for young, body
conscious streety stuff: John
Richmond, Roser Marcé, Hilary
Bockham, Angel UK, World
Service and other poised-on-the-
brink young designers; also shoes
and accessories. Sizes 10 to 14 (but
you had better be all muscle); prices
reasonable (£50.00 plus). Also sell
for chaps.

....

Knitwear

HYNE & EAMES
299 Cannongate
Royal Mile
Edinburgh EH8 8BQ
031 557 4056

Open: 10.30 to 5.30 Mon. to Sat.
Credit Cards: Access, American
Express, Diners Club, Visa

Small, one floor bazaar-like shop –
all bright colours, display baskets
and sofas to relax on; sells original
fashion knitwear separates with a
traditional element (updated Fair
Isle for example) but very modern
styling. Mainly shetland wool, but
some lambswool and botany wool.
Pay £80.00 for a short, bumfreezer
style cardi, up to £160.00 for a coat.
Co-ordinating hats made by local
designer from knitted panels in
diverting shapes – stove pipes for
example. Also scarves, unusual

leather bags and jewellery.
Halfway between the Castle and
Holyrood Palace, they naturally
attract a large tourist trade, but the
local following is very strong.
Excellent stuff – they also sell to
New York and Paris.

....

Shoes

JUNE JOHNSTON
5 William Street
Edinburgh
031 225 3663

Open: 10.00 to 6.00 Mon to Fri;
10.00 to 5.00 Sat.
Credit Cards: Access, Visa

Small shop selling chic Italian
shoes: Pancaldi, Baldinini, Arcus in
sizes 3 to 8½/9. Prices range from
£35.00 to £150.00. Jolly accessories:
Dents gloves, Enny bags, Angie
Gooderham jewellery. Satin shoes
and bags can be dyed (via Anello
and Davide).

....

Special Sizes

THE EXTRA INCH
16 William Street
Edinburgh
031 226 3303

Open: 9.30 to 5.30 Mon. to Fri; 9.30
to 1.00 Sat.
Credit Cards: Access, American
Express, Visa

The best shop for larger sizes in the
north of the United Kingdom:
people fly in from Cardiff and
Manchester to shop here. Warm
chocolate and gold outside leads to
cool classic cream within, where
hangs their speciality: probably the
largest selection of exclusive
German and Italian dresses and
separates for special occasions.
Prices from £70.00 up (top whack
for the lovely couture numbers)
sizes 16 to 26. Downstairs is an
intriguing subterranean sprawl of
four rooms each dedicated to
different kinds of smart daywear
and separates. They have the
Martha Schreck collection of bright
colourful summer clothes; last year
the bermuda shorts sold like gelati
in July, so more are planned this
year. A seamstress on the premises
makes free alterations.

GLASGOW

BLONDES
18 Wilson Street
Glasgow G1 15S
041 552 3946

Open: 10.30 to 5.30 Mon. to Sat.
Credit Cards: Access, American
Express, Visa

Streetwise clothes from Comme
par Hazard, Le Garage, Transit,
Rocco Barocco, Maggie Calhoun,
Wet, Twisted Sister, Nieuw
Amsterdam Peil, Diane Gilman.
Soon starting up their own label
(Blondes) with fashion jodhpurs,
tops etc. Sizes 8 to 14; lots of hot
Salsa while you pose.

CRUISE
43 Renfield Street
Glasgow
041 552 0034

Open: 10.00 to 6.00 Mon. to Fri;
9.30 to 6.00 Sat.
Credit Cards: Access, American
Express, Diners Club, Visa

Strictly for slender young things:
they do have some 14s, but...fun
affordable club clothes from Soap
Studio, Mathilde, Nicola Georgiou
and other young up and coming
designers. Leather jackets, denim,
and accessories. Chaps' clothes and
accessories at numbers 39 and 41
Renfield Street. There is another
Cruise in EDINBURGH.

CAMPUS
3 to 5 Gibson Street
Glasgow
041 334 6862

Open: 9.30 to 5.30 Mon. to Fri; 9.00
to 6.00 Sat.
Credit Cards: Access, American
Express, Diners Club, Visa

Dark eccentric shop, all gilt mirrors
and mahogany; clothes displayed
dramatically on black and gold
cartwheels and a rocking sheep for
children. Jean Muir, KL,
Ginochietti and the Academy
Collection from Betty Davis,
doing stylish things to traditional
Scottish fabrics like tweed and
tartan. Eccentric intellectual hats.
Sizes 8 to 16, prices from affordable
to expensive; six month charge
account available. The Academy
Collection is available at 39
Hanover Street, Edinburgh.
    There are also Campuses at
EDINBURGH and OXFORD.

ICHI NI SAN
123 Candleriggs
Glasgow
G1 1NP
041 552 2545

Open: 10.00 to 6.00 Mon. to Sat.
Credit Cards: Access, American
Express, Diners Club, Visa

Rapidly becoming more of a tourist
attraction than a retail operation,
Ichi Ni San is high chic (distressed
walls, agonized metalwork) in the
ultra cred part of town, the old
merchant city quarter. They sell
top of the range interesting

GLASGOW, CITY OF CHIC
····

If you want to buy a decent
frock, go to Glasgow; it's got all
the labels, all the shops, and
none of the bored
condescension you get from
most London designer
shop assistants.
····
Princes Square
(Buchanan Street) would not
look out of place in Milan: all
sandstone, glass and
colonnades and the best shops.
Cross over Argyle Street to St
Enoch's Centre, a breathtaking
new shopping 'high street'
enclosed in a huge Gaudiesque
glass dome. A little further east
is the Merchant City Quarter,
(Wilson Street, Glassford
Street, Candleriggs) home of
designer cred.
····
Glaswegians really know how
to dress up: shops sell much
more formal and party wear
here than in the south.
····

---

designer labels (fashion punster
Moschino, wonderful Christine
Ahrens shoes, all the other
stylocrats) with prices in the
stratosphere to match. However,
once you have penetrated the
intimidating portals, the staff are
friendly and well informed. It may
help to know that Ichi Ni San is
nothing more intimidating than 1–
2–3 in Japanese.

MOON
The Studio
519 Great Western Road
Glasgow G12 8HN
041 339 2315

Open: 9.30 to 5.30 Mon. to Fri;
10.00 to 6.00 Sat.
Credit Cards: Access, Visa

Small square shop tucked away off
the main road, housed in a pretty
Victorian tea room. There are no
shop windows, but a huge glass
dome on top, so Moon is a bit of a
secret; shopping there has a
gratifyingly conspiratorial feel.
Very restful, cream walls and
woodwork, staircase to a little
gallery; squidgy sofas to sit on. Run
with quiet and considered
efficiency by Annie Good, an ex-
librarian with a flair for repose. She
keeps things exclusive by stocking
only three of each style in sizes 10 to
14 (alterations available); top range
is Paul Costelloe, Nicole Farhi, KL,
Ralph Lauren Polo, Ally Capellino;
younger cheaper range includes
Fenn, Wright & Manson,
WilliWear and floaty clothes from
Dorin Frankfurt. Small range of
Mulberry accessories. Regular
customers are on the extensive
mailing list, and are first to know
about the new season's lines.

....

SAXS
36/37 Princes Square
48 Buchanan Street
Glasgow
041 221 2487

Open: 9.30 to 6.00 Mon. to Sat.
Credit Cards: Access, American
Express, Diners Club, Visa, Saxs
own card

As blissful as the BRIGHTON shop,
but able to carry more formal and
elaborate clothes (eg Anthony
Price) as the Scots have a much
firmer grip on dressing up for
occasions than the sloppy, seditious
southerners. Grown up
sophisticated clothes (Ginochietti,
Moschino, Ozbek, GianFranco
Ferre, Montana, Romeo Gigli,
Versace etc) and younger more
casual stuff (Hamnett II, Sara
Sturgeon, Junior Gaultier, Betty
Jackson, Ben de Lisi); sizes 8 to 16,
prices £50.00 to £600.00. The
owner (Hamid Ameri, with a
wondrous ponytail) shuttles
between Glasgow and Brighton
stores. Friendly, informed staff;
regular clientele includes the
Connollys and other media
mighty.

....

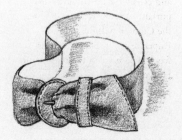

THE WAREHOUSE
61–65 Glassford Street
Glasgow G1 1UG
041 552 4181

Open: 10.00 to 6.00 Mon.to Sat.
Credit Cards: Access, American
Express, Diners Club, Visa

Just refurbished, The Warehouse is
three floors of crucial fashion:
young club clothes in the basement,
chaps on ground floor, girls on top.
Huge range of mouthwatering
stuff: Rifat Ozbek, O for Ozbek,
Jean Paul Gaultier and Junior
Gaultier, Sara Sturgeon, Katherine
Hamnett, Myrène de Prémonville
Studio, Ghost, Karen Boyd,
Workers for Freedom, Rocco
Barocco and many more in size 8 to
14 (alterations available); gorgeous
shoes from Christine Ahrens,
Emma Hope, Jean Claude Bidi,
Martine Sitbon; hats from
Bernstock and Spiers; jewellery to
die for from New York bead king
Eric Beamon and our own Dinny
Hall. When frock fatigue sets in,
there is a stylish caff with the best
cappucino in Glasgow and ace food
– the Saturday meeting place for the
Glasgow glitterati.

Clothes from The Warehouse are
much in demand for films and TV,
and celebs cluster about its airy
portals – Joanne Whalley-Kilmer,
the Connollys Billy and Pam,
Rupert Everett; Simple Minds
frocked up here for their next tour.
Heaven.

MCDONALD MACKAY (KILTMAKERS) LTD
105 HOPE STREET
GLASGOW G2 611
041 204 3930

Open: 8.30 to 5.30 Mon. to Sat.
Credit Cards: Access, Diners
Club, Visa

Kilts and full Highland rig can
be bought or hired from here.
Women's skirts and kilts
made to measure and a
worldwide mail order service
(just the thing for your aunt
in Fiji).

····

If you are ineligible for a
tartan, go for the Culture
Tartan specially created for
1990.

····

YVETTE WINOCOUR
7 McClaren Place
Clarkston Road
Glasgow
041 637 1902

Open: 10.00 to 5.00 Mon. to Sat.
Credit Cards: Access, American
Express, Diners Club, Visa

Well established shop, providing
high profile fashion long before
Glasgow became synonymous
with chic. Good expensive labels;
Georges Rech, Jean Muir, Jean
Muir Studio, Paul Costelloe, Trixie
Schober; knitwear from Edina
Ronay, Krizia Poi, Joy and Fun.
Also accessories, hats and bags.
Wardrobe planning and alterations.

Hats

THE HAT SHOP
30 Wilson Street
Glasgow
041 553 2469

Open: 10.00 to 6.00 Mon. to Fri;
late (7.00) on Thurs; 10.00 to 5.30
Sat.
Credit Cards: Access, Visa

Part of The Hat Shop triumvirate
(the other two are in London).
Wonderful own brand hats for men
and women; prices range from
about £10.00 upwards. Sales are
excellent (bottom of the range
straw for about £4.00). The Hat
Shop also understands that some
people have large heads.... They
will also make up customers' own
fabric.

Jewellery

BUTLER & WILSON
33 Princes Square
Glasgow
041 204 0980

Open: 9.30 to 5.30 Mon. to Sat.
Credit Cards: Access, American
Express, Diners Club, Visa

Naturally, the chicest costume
jewellers have a presence in the
chicest city in the land. The
expected range of house designed
silver and paste jewellery. Prices go
from reasonable to expensive.

Lingerie

BRIEF ENCOUNTER
27 Clarence Drive
Hyndland
Glasgow
041 357 2383

Open: 9.30 to 6.00 Mon. to Sat.
Credit Cards: Access, American
Express, Diners Club, Visa

Original mahogany fittings and
glass cases in this small shop selling
Lejaby, Louis Feraud, David
Napier, Lisel Charmel lingerie and
swimwear from Fantasy,
Rassurelle, Rosch, Gideon
Oberson and Louis Feraud again.
Bras from the flat to the alpine (32aa
to 40g); swimwear 10 to 44,
nighties 10 to 22. Trained fitters (a
dying breed) will help you choose
the right support: most of us wear
the wrong size bras all our lives.

THE BARRAS
····
244 Gallowgate
Glasgow G4 0TS
····
Sats & Suns 9.00 to 5.00
····
Glasgow's famous market: a
must – over 1000 stallholders
selling everything and
anything and charming the
money out of your pockets
with inimitable patter.
····

WALES

●●●●●●●●●●

For the country that gave the world Laura
Ashley, Wales is curiously muted on the
fashion front. Even so, go to Cardiff for
adventurous design and young fun
clothes; Swansea for grown-up dressing
and crucial surfie wear; Cowbridge for
serious frocks and serious rocks; and
North Wales for that very attractive
Celtic phenomenon, the Craft Centre,
selling well-designed and very affordable
fashion alongside beautiful
locally made artefacts.

ABERGAVENNY

BLONDIES
34 Frogmore Street
Abergavenny
0878 77808

Open: 9.30 to 5.30 Mon. to Fri.
Credit Cards: Access, American
Express, Diners Club, Visa

Wearable mid price and mid range
labels for the professional woman:
Jacques Vert, Pola and other
eurowear. Sizes 8 to 18.

....

Mady Gerrard
is an exotic Hungarian born
designer who specializes in big,
spectacular jackets in unusual
materials – leather, silk,
patchwork, quilted silk.
····
She has made stagewear for
Shirley Bassey, and so has a
strong grasp on the
theatrical.
····
Jackets cost around £300.00 to
order; if you want to make a
dramatic entrance contact her at

31 Enterprise Park
Enterprise Way
Newport, Gwent NP9 2AQ
····

JUNGLES
6 High Street
Abergavenny
0873 4888

Open: 9.00 to 5.30 Mon. to Sat.
Credit Cards: Access, Visa

Lively shop that combines
interesting affordable offbeat
fashion with upmarket gifts from
the likes of Crabtree and Evelyn.
The deceptively cunning
marketing ploy is to fill the front
part of the shop with fun inflatables
and *objets daft* to divert the attention
of children and chaps; then
whoever's buying can look at the
clothes in relative calm and peace.
Monsoon, InWear, Adini, OuiSet,
Oilily, Fenn, Wright & Manson
and Mexx in sizes 8 to 14. Shoes
from Anello and Davide and Zoo
(sizes 3 to 8). Bags, belts, velvet
berets. Jungles is owned by Philip
and Poppy Cochran, whose other
lively establishments include
Noyadd Rhulens in BRECON,
Lettuce & Mulberry in
ABERYSTWYTH and Blue Leader in
HEREFORD.

....

ABERYSTWYTH

LETTUCE & MULBERRY
16–18 Pier Street
Aberystwyth
0970 625583

Open: 9.00 to 5.30 Mon. to Sat.
Credit Cards: Access, Visa

Latest of the Cochran shops; very large single storey selling the wearable affordable casuals from InWear, French Connection, Monsoon, Adini, Fenn Wright & Manson etc; shoes from Anello and Davide and Zoo. See Noyadd Rhulans Country Store BRECON, Jungles ABERGAVENNY and Blue Leader HEREFORD.

BRECON

NOYADD RHULANS
COUNTRY STORE
46 High Street
Brecon
0874 5259

Open: 9.30 to 5.00 Mon. to Sat.
Credit Cards: Access, Visa

Part of the Philip and Poppy Cochran empire. Jolly, affordable clothes (French Connection, Adini, InWear, Monsoon, Java etc) shoes from Anello and Davide and Zoo. The largest of the Cochran fleet, this store has three floors and also sells dress fabrics. See also Jungles in ABERGAVENNY, Lettuce & Mulberry in ABERYSTWYTH and Blue Leader in HEREFORD.

CRAFTY DRESSING
····

The CRAFTCENTRE CYMRU combines classic fashionable clothes with beautiful local crafts: luminous tweeds and thick dark honey side by side. Penmachno Mill, Penmachno, Betwys-y-Coed (0690 2545), is open from Easter to late Autumn, seven days a week. Watch the tweed and wool being made (designed by Beryl Gibson, textile designer to Betty Jackson and Ralph Lauren), then snap up jackets, skirts, caps and scarves; lovely cafe here too. All clothes are own design and exclusive – Laura Ashley style at half the price – liberty print skirts and appliqued tops (sizes 10 to 16/18); lovely knitwear at great prices (start around £30.00) from Welsh whizz Alison Taylor and an exclusive collection by Carrie White (who also designs for Geordie Knit maestros Penny Plain, see page 155). Craftcentre Cymru shops at High Street, BALA, 7a Castle Ditch, CAERNARVON, Castle Street, CONWAY, and wonderful new Harbour Shop, Madoc Harbour, PORTHMADOG – all brooding welsh slate and untamed wood. There is also a non-cymru branch in St Michael's Row CHESTER, where the label is kindly translated as Traditions of Wales.
····

CARDIFF

BODY BASICS
79 Pontcanna Street
Cardiff
0222 397025

Open: 10.00 to 6.30 Mon. to Sat.
Credit Cards: Access, American
Express, Diners Club, Visa

The owner of this splendid shop is
Lisa Karamouzis, ex-buyer for
Joseph, and her own venture is not
unlike the old Chinese laundry –
black and white and chrome and
wood. She believes in smart clothes
which can take you anywhere with
the addition of a few right
accessories and her shop is stocked
with delicious KL, YSL, Sara
Sturgeon, Moschino and Monica
Chong casual wear and separates
(sizes 8 to 14). Quite expensive, but
wonderfully wearable anywhere.
Accessories, jewellery and
intriguing designer gadgets and
lifewear such as gleaming chrome
Alessi kettles.

HUDSON & HUDSON
16 Queens West Centre
Queen Street
Cardiff CF1 4BU
0222 226300

Open: 9.30 to 5.30 Mon. to Fri; 9.30
to 6.00 Sat.
Credit Cards: Access, American
Express, Diners Club, Visa; own
Hudson & Hudson card

Great airy spacious shop, all glass
and white marbling. Fiendishly
cunning display units makes the
clothes appear to be hovering rather
than hanging up; punchy young
labels for both sexes – Ghost, Exile,
Shirley Wong, Charlotte Smith,
Extravert for affordable high
fashion (expect to pay between
£100.00 and £200.00 for an outfit).
Sizes 10 to 14. Fun shop with pop
vids running on strategically placed
monitors.

  Also in BRISTOL.

HOBBY AND CRACKERS
37 Morgan Arcade
Cardiff
0222 228142

Open: 10.00 to 5.30 Mon. to Sat.
Credit Cards: Access, American
Express, Diners Club, Visa;
interest free credit scheme

Hobby and Crackers are now
united to make two selling floors.
Clothes to build the wardrobe of
25+ professionals. Impeccable
labels: Bitte, Georges Rech, Harry
Who, Krizia, Betty Jackson, Bruce
Oldfield 1992, Bleu Blanc Rouge.
Evening wear from Carole Lee.
Sizes 8 to 14 (on site alterations
available). Jewellery by Angie
Gooderham. Excellent personal
service.

CARMARTHEN

MORSE CODE
27–28 Blue Street
Carmarthen
0267 234384

Open: 9.00 to 5.30 Mon. to Sat.
Credit Cards: Access, American
Express, Diners Club, Visa

The non-nuptial outpost of Morse
Code in SWANSEA. Carries the same
swanky labels (KL, YSL, Valiano,
Caroline Charles etc) and is
therefore good hunting ground for
high earning career women. Sizes 8
to 16.

....

COWBRIDGE

RAGGS
23 High Street
Cowbridge
04463 2046

Open: 9.45 to 5.30 Mon. to Sat.
Credit Cards: Access, American
Express, Diners Club, Visa

Pretty shop on two floors in an
attractive old building. Excellent
upmarket labels: Gale Hoppen
dressy suits; Paul Costelloe's
Dressage (and matching hats);
Mani, Gaston Jaunet, Thierry
Mugler, Salmon & Green,
Strenesse, Fenn, Wright & Manson
among others in sizes 8 to 14. Also
Joan Biggs hats and good selection
of costume jewellery and belts.
Coffee is offered; regular customers
come for the excellent service.

....

Jewellery

JENNY WREN
23 High Street
Cowbridge
04463 4165

Open: 10.00 to 5.30 Mon. to Sat.
Credit Cards: Access, American
Express, Diners Club, Visa

Very upmarket jewellers selling
serious silver and gold and real
rocks. Lots of collars and earrings
in high fashion designs, and classic
Italian stuff. Small amount of
antique jewellery and a fun range
(£40.00 to £100.00) Folli Follie
which sells like mad (well it would,
wouldn't it...)

....

SWANSEA

GOOD HABIT
7–8 Nelson Street
Swansea SA1 3QE
0792 461606

Open: 9.30 to 5.30 Mon. to Sat.
Credit Cards: Access, American
Express, Diners Club, Visa

Jolly shop with elephant logo
selling very affordable, ethnicy
separates: Monsoon, Java, French
Connection plus their own Good
Habit label from Bali: bright batik
prints on cotton and cotton jersey
baggy pants, big shirts and jackets
(sizes 10 to 16); also big one-size T-
shirts and swimwear. There is also
a surfwear department (lots of
surfies in Swansea) with crucial
labels: Ocean Pacific, Hot Tuna.

....

VANIA JESMOND
89 Bryn–y-Mor Road
Swansea SA1 4JE
0792 461165

Open: 9.30 to 5.30 Mon. to Sat;
closes at 1.00 Thurs.
Credit Cards: Access, American
Express, Diners Club, Visa

Large chic shop dotted with sofas
and mags for non-participating
husbands. Pricey chic labels (Mani,
MaxMara, Vittadini, Bleu Blanc
Rouge, Zucchero) in size 8 to 16.
New collections come in every
month, and so there is a great
choice for the professional high
earner. Expect to pay £100.00 up,
£600.00 or so for an ensemble; they
have a six month interest free credit
scheme.

....

MORSE CODE
5 Caer Street
Castle Gardens
Swansea
0792 654625

Open: 9.00 to 5.30 Mon. to Sat.
Credit Cards: Access, American
Express, Diners Club, Visa

The downstairs bridal department,
rustling with over 300 silk designer
wedding frocks is world famous;
people come from countries away,
and prospective brides are offered
wine, coffee, champagne and even
sandwiches if they have come from
very far away.

Upstairs is the fashion floor;
expensive elegant labels: Caroline
Charles, Salvatore Ferragamo,
YSL, Valiano, Trixie Schober,

Etienne Aigner; knitwear from
Edina Ronay, shirts from The
Shirtmaker. Just right for the
honeymoon trousseau and for
mothers of the bride who don't
want to look like mothers of the
bride. Prices suit the labels; sizes 8
to 16, and there is an alteration
service. There is also a shop in
CARMARTHEN, but it does not carry
the bridal range.

....

THE MARINA COLLECTION
18 Ocean Crescent
Swansea SA1 1YZ
0792 644766

Open: 10.00 to 5.30 Mon. to Sat.
Credit Cards: Access, American
Express, Diners Club, Visa

Breathtaking, if occasionally
windswept, site on the new
Swansea Marina houses an
exclusive collection of labels not
available anywhere else in Swansea:
the Emmanuels, Xandra Rhodes,
Sporting Life, Hauber, Roots
(smart separates). Sizes 8 to 18.
Some people drop in by boat.

....

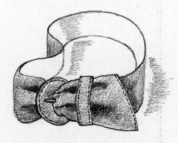

IRELAND

....

Only Southern Ireland really; avant-
garde northerners come to Dublin for
fashion breaks, and it is to Dublin you
go for irresistible chic presented with
irresistible charm. Cork is for relaxed
fashion: although it is a city, it would
really rather be a big town. The Avoca
Phenomenon almost covers the country.
Remember that wherever there is a
romantic lakebound castle, there will
probably be a handcraft centre selling
delicious knits and linen. And there are
cafés everywhere.

THE AVOCA STORY
....
Avoca Weavers
(they want to drop the clumsy Handweavers handle)
were founded in Avoca in 1723, and are therefore the oldest weaving establishment in Ireland (which takes some doing). They are now a thriving multi million £ concern. Banish instantly from your mind the notion of worthy porridge coloured matting; Avoca weave magic with lightweight wool, worsted and mohair to produce luminous, diaphanous tweeds in jewel bright colours.

They make these up into jackets, skirts, capes, shawls, suits, and dresses, which sell like hot cakes worldwide. For £70.00 to £140.00, you get quality fabric, timeless design and clothes that look just that little bit unusual.
....
The label is Avoca Collection, sizes are 8 to 22.
Men's clothes too.
Avoca shops at AVOCA, BRAY, BUNRATTY, LETTERFRACK and in England, BATH.
Mail order from BRAY.
....

AVOCA

AVOCA WEAVERS
Avoca
Co Wicklow
001 353 402 5105

Open: 9.00 to 6.00 Mon. to SUNDAY
Credit Cards: Access, American Express, Diners Club, Visa

Where it all started; a little village at the foot of the Wicklow Mountains, not far from major tourist stopover, Glendalough. This is the original Avoca mill, complete with millstream, and it is still the powerhouse of the Avoca operation. You can look around the mill before browsing through the clothes; there is a cafe to restore you after decision making. Local crafts also on offer include interesting pottery from nearby Arklow.

Other Avocas at BRAY, BUNRATTY, LETTERFRACK and BATH.

BRAY

AVOCA WEAVERS
Kilmacanogue
Bray
Co Wicklow
0001 867466

Open: 9.00 to 5.30 Mon. to SUNDAY
Credit Cards: Access, American Express, Diners Club, Visa

Head office and brand new shop of the wonderful Avoca Handweavers (they are trying to drop the cumbersome handweavers handle): luminous wool classics; traditional Irish knits and local crafts. Wonderful cafe. Contact this shop for annual mail order catalogue. See box opposite. Other Avoca shops at AVOCA, BUNRATTY, LETTERFRACK and BATH.

BUNRATTY

AVOCA WEAVERS
Bunratty Castle
County Clare
010 353 61 4364029

Open: 9.00 to 6.00 Mon. to SUNDAY
Credit Cards: Access, American Express, Diners Club, Visa

Yes, a real castle; the Handcrafts Centre is opposite the famous watering hole, Dirty Nelly's. The distinctive range of bright tweeds expanded by an excellent range of Irish knitwear and wonderful pure silk blouses (about £200.00) from Vonnie Reynolds. This Avoca has recently been wondrously refurbished and expanded and now features a lunch room. See also AVOCA, BRAY, LETTERFRACK and BATH.

CORK

RICHARD ALAN
63 Oliver Plunkett Street
Cork
010 353 21273759

Open: 9.00 to 5.30 Mon. to Sat.
Credit Cards: Access, American Express, Diners Club, Visa

A second branch of the speciality label store in DUBLIN, carrying much the same high octane designer stock.

MONICA JOHN
French Church Street
Cork
010 353 21271399

Open: 9.00 to 6.00 Mon to Sat.
Credit Cards: Access, American Express, Diners Club, Visa

A lovely old shop in the heart of a spanky new up and coming area (restaurants, upmarket glassware shops); the same range as the DUBLIN shop – much French and a lot of dressy Germans – but also main and Dressage collections from your man Costelloe.

OTOKIO 2
Kinsale
Cork

Credit Cards: Access, American Express, Diners Club, Visa

A branch of the palace of hip chic in DUBLIN; same crucial labels (Hamnett, Lainey Keogh, Boyd & Storey etc) and similar jolly fun.
    As we went to press, this shop was moving premises, and the telephone number was unavailable.

DUBLIN

RICHARD ALAN
58 Grafton Street
Dublin
0001 775149

Open: 9.00 to 5.30 Mon. to Sat.
Credit Cards: Access, American
Express, Diners Club, Visa

Tall, elegant Dublin town house
full of elegant speciality fashion.
Friendly, intimate atmosphere in
which to browse through
scrumptious collections: top guns
Genny, Ungaro, Mani, Valentino,
Roland Klein; lots of fashion
Germans (Escada, L'Estelle, Fink,
Hucke, Betty Barclay, Laurel); mid
price French casuals; easy to wear
classics from Quaker. Lots more in
sizes 10 to 16 spread over 2 floors.
Twelve helpful staff and in-house
alterations. A pocket Harvey
Nichols in the heart of Bloomland
(St Stephen's Green is but a step
away).
    Another Richard Alan in CORK.

BROWN THOMAS
Grafton Street
Dublin
0001 795666

Open: 9.30 to 6.00 Mon. to Sat; late
(8.00) Thurs.
Credit Cards: Access, American
Express, Diners Club, Visa

Huge, gorgeous and plush; the
Harrods of Baille Atha Cliath
(Dublin to you). Three floors of
well organized frocks. First floor
for mainline fashion; International
designer Room (Genny, Byblos,
MaxMara, Adriano Vittadini,
Marella and more); Private Lives
boutique with Arabella Pollen,
Jean Muir main and Studio, Edina
Ronay, Sonia Rykiel; partywear
from Bellville Sassoon; major Irish
input of course: Richard Lewis,
John Rocha, Michelina Stacpoole,
Louise Kennedy (Irish Designer of
the Year 1989) and, naturally, P.
Costelloe main collection and
Dressage. Less expensive euro
section – Mondi, Basler, Jobis; also
stalwarts Jaeger and Viyella. Great
range of Patrizia big clothes (12 to
22). Most ranges cover sizes 8 to 16,
alterations possible. Downstairs for
high flying ultrachic in-shop shops:
Gucci Boutique and Ralph Lauren.
Gorgeous designer costume
jewellery in the Bijou section, and a
Hat Gallery. Food halls and
restaurants. Unmissable.

THE DESIGN CENTRE
Powers Court Town House
Centre
Clarendon Street
Dublin 2
0001 795718

Open: 9.30 to 6.00 Mon. to Sat.
Credit Cards: Access, American
Express, Diners Club, Visa

Powers Court is a glitzy Trocadero
style shopping plaza; The Design
Centre, on the first floor, is a huge
bright shop, a giant upmarket
Hyper Hyper, showcasing new
Irish design exclusively. More than
20 represented from the embryonic
to the established. Loads of hand
knits: Lainey Keogh's avant garde

garb – amazing shapes and boggling yarns combos (not for nothing did she win the C. Lacroix Designer award 1989) – plus her new crochet collection (expect to pay around £300.00); pretty pastels and patterns from Dorothy Ronan on the ultra feminine Hot Dot label; summer cotton cables and matching skirts from Lynn Elliott on the Lyn-Mar label. For clothes, there is top smartie Louise Kennedy (very tailored and Armaniesque); amazing acts with linens, including the hottest hooded jackets (around £165.00) from Mairead Whistler; and very ahead-of-the game stuff from Pink Ink, a Northern Ireland design team who have settled this side of the border. The Design Centre also features an Innovative Section, in which it nurtures the talents of newly hatched fashion college grads – they get to sell their stuff and learn the cold hard facts about retailing at the same time; the idea is that when they are successful and confident they will take up one of the shop units. This one is for serious fashion addicts.

MONICA JOHN
William Elliott Store
Wicklow Street
Dublin
0001 794290

Open: 9.00 to 6.00 Mon. to Sat.
Credit Cards: Access, American Express, Diners Club, Visa

Smart shop that fronts onto the street and so keeps niftily aloof from the shopping centre of which it is part. Lovely clothes: Georges

---

LACE IN THE LOUGHS
· · · ·
Ashford Castle stands on an island in the Lough Mask, County Mayo; in the distance lies Lough Corrib, in County Galway.
This dreamy, watergirt place in open to the public in the summer months and there is a shopeen in the dungeons where you can buy exquisite blouses, hand-made from antique linen and ancient lace.
Oh, the romance of it all....
· · · ·
Ashford Castle Boutique
Ashford Castle
Cong
County Mayo
010 353 92 46003
· · · ·

Rech and Synonyme, Rodier, lots of effortlessly chic French casuals (Le Sport etc); very strong on Miss Antoinette, a German range of snazzy little silky dresses and dressy separates in bright jewelly colours: the Irish, like the Scots and women from Northern England really understand how to dress up for an occasion. Sizes 8 through 18 (although not in all labels) and alterations. Very helpful staff.
Another Monica John in CORK.

OTOKIO
3 South Ann Street
Dublin
0001 777325

Open: 9.00 to 6.00 Mon. to Sat;
late (8.00) Thurs.
Credit Cards: Access, American
Express, Diners Club, Visa

Sublime, hardcore chic:
monochrome decor, Eileen Gray
chairs and irresistible to media
persons and arties. Strong editorial
grip on the labels: Katharine
Hamnett, Dolce and Gabbana,
Fujiwara, Adolpho Dominguez,
Boyd & Storey (together and as
individuals). Sizes 8 to 14.
Gorgeous wacky knitwear from
ace Irish designer Lainey Keogh,
winner of 1989's Christian Lacroix
Designer Award. Aloof is not
Dublin style, and this is a very
friendly shop run by Des
O'Connor (no, don't say it) and his
wife Marianne. Great place for hero
spotting: bald primadonna Sinead
O'Connor, the Connollys (when
they're not in Glasgow), the
mighty U2 (can this be where The
Edge gets his hats?). Two more
shops: Otokio 2 in CORK; and
another, more casual shop (InWear,
KH, some kids stuff) in Church
Square, Monaghan.

LETTERFRACK

CONNEMARA
HANDCRAFTS
Letterfrack
Connemara
010 353 9541058

Open: Easter until late Autumn;
9.30 to 5.30/6.00 Mon. to Sat.
Credit Cards: Access, American
Express, Diners Club, Visa

Part of the Avoca empire, with the
range expanded to include the
romantic muted misty Connemara
tweeds. Also immaculate local
handknits, and enormous range of
crafts: paintings, wall hangings,
silverware, pottery, all carefully
selected, coffee shop, of course.
Probably the best of the Irish
handcraft centres, certainly one of
the most beautiful, on the wild
Atlantic coast. The arrival of WB
Yeats treading softly on someone's
dreams would not be a surprise.
    Other Avocas at AVOCA, BRAY,
BUNRATTY and BATH.

NAAS

CLICKS
6 North Main Street
Naas
Co Kildare
010 353 4579568

Open: 10.00 to 6.00 Mon. to Sat.
Credit Cards: Access, American
Express, Diners Club, Visa

Smart green and cream shop run by
Callista Devine, giving a very
personal service: clothes for
snappy-dressing working women
(Naas is a commuter town about 20
minutes from Dublin): Feraud,
Mimmina, Gardeur, Jerry Webber,
Basler and major German input in
sizes 10 to 16. Frank Usher party
frocks. Some costume jewellery.

MAIL ORDER

· · · · · · · · · ·

For the rusticated, isolated or housebound, mail order is literally a godsend. The big league catalogue 'department stores' are well known, as are their clothes-only spin-offs. The following short selection offers something slightly different in knitwear, shoes, accessories and unusual garments.

Clothes

ONE OF GILLIE'S
Llantrithyd
Cowbridge
South Glamorgan CF7 7UB
04468 357

Very intriguing. Skirts, jackets,
dresses, pants and swimwear
(bikinis and costumes) made to
order. When you send for a
catalogue, you receive a set of clear
drawings of basic shapes (including
back views) which can be swapped
about; also a card of fabric samples.
Then you plan your own
wardrobe. Simple really. Shapes
are good and uncluttered, sizes 8 to
20 (except for some swimwear),
prices acceptable considering the
fabric quality (silk, silk jersey, wool
crepe). The bikinis are particularly
useful, as you can order any top to
go with any bottom.

Bags

CARPET BAGS
2&3 Fourwheel Drive
Rougham Industrial Estate
Bury St Edmunds
IP30 9ND
0359 70825

And now for something quite
different. Huge range of carpet and
tapestry bags – purses, folios,
briefcases, handbags, Gladstone
bags, tote bags, spec cases, real
luggage – at very reasonable prices.
The carpet is lightweight and the
tapestry is specially laminated to
prevent grime build-up. Also

available are dashing tapestry
waistcoats for men and women
(around £50.00). Very Beau
Brummell.

Knitwear

PENNY PLAIN
10 Marlborough Crescent
Newcastle on Tyne NE1 4EE
091 232 1124

Designer knitwear. Lovely
substantial catalogue full of
beautiful hand framed knits –
jumpers, cardies and lovely shaped
jackets – from Sue Cutting, Carrie
White, Sophie Schellenberg; prices
range from £50.00 upwards, sizes
s, m and l. Also an exclusive Kaffe
Fassett collection. If you are on a
Fassett-free budget, look at the
Peppercorn Collection, unusual
knits at around £35.00. Well chosen
(and sensibly photographed)
collection of sterling silver costume
jewellery; also leather bags and
sensible skirts.

There is a Penny Plain shop in St
Mary's Place, Newcastle, which
sells much of the range plus extra
jewellery.

COTSWOLD WOOLLENS
2 Queen's Circus
Cheltenham
Gloucestershire GL50 1RX
0242 226262

Write or phone for a splendid
colour brochure (two a year).
Cotswold Woollens knitwear for
men and women at very reasonable

prices (£20.00 to £50.00) and lots of jolly designs: classic fair isle, delicate flower designs, wacky Ruperts and Parrots, strong abstract colour patterns; all sizes s, m and l. Matching socks. They also have a small range of cord or viyella skirts (sizes 10 to 18) in lovely colours to team with the jumpers and dashing sloany striped shirts (s, m and l). Plain lambswool scarves and big spotty hankies for running away from home with. All clothes also available at their various shops (see below). Shops in Dudley and Stratford on Avon planned.

....

BATH
5 Upper Borough Walls
Bath
Avon
0225 446829

....

BOURTON ON THE WATER
High Street
Bourton on the Water
Gloucestershire
0451 22340

....

BROADWAY
Cotswold Court
Broadway
Hereford & Worcester
0386 858056

....

CHIPPING CAMPDEN
High Street
Chipping Campden
Gloucestershire
0386 840965

....

CHELTENHAM
Regent Arcade
Cheltenham
Gloucestershire
0242 224693

....

CIRENCESTER
Market Place
Cirencester
Gloucestershire
0285 658555

....

HEREFORD
41 Broad Street
Hereford
Hereford & Worcester
0432 264351

....

LUDLOW
15 King Street
Ludlow
Shropshire
0584 5612

....

SHREWSBURY
13 The Square
Shrewsbury
Shropshire
0743 67663

....

Shoes

CRISPINS BY POST
Royal Exchange Shopping Arcade
St Ann's Square,
Manchester M2 7DB
061 833 0022

Shoes by post; send for the catalogue for the range. Specialists in very narrow shoes (AAA).

....

FASHION CHAINLETS

· · · · · · · · · ·

Bridging the gap between the multiples and franchises on the one hand and the indies on the other is a group of small chains of clothes and shoe shops which deliver fashion impact but can afford to trim the price a little.

Clothes

ANOKHI

Anokhi started up 20 years ago importing clothes based on the traditional textile skills of India. Hand made dyes, hand printed fabrics and hand embroidery is provided by small workshops and co-operatives; in return, Anokhi supply cash flow, design and marketing expertise. The result is a range of airy, easy to wear clothes in the Monsoon mode: ethnic with a cutting fashion edge: this season for instance sees wide black and white voile pants with co-ordinating black waistcoat tops. Prices are good: outfits for around £40.00 and sizes 10 to 16, though loose styles and elastic waists will accommodate the extra inch or so.

Anokhi sell wholesale to outlets nationwide, and also have a small chain of own name shops, jolly with turquoise and warm wood. All shops open from 10.00 to 6.00 Mon. to Sat. and all take major credit cards.

London Anokhis:
22 Wellington Street
London WC2
071 836 0663

192 Fulham Road
London SW10
071 351 5076

Other Anokhis:
HOME COUNTIES

4 The Square
Richmond
Surrey
081 948 3302

60 North Street
Guildford
Surrey
0483 303829

THE WEST COUNTRY

23 West Market Place
Cirencester
Gloucestershire
0285 658261

EAST ANGLIA

3 St Mary's Passage
Cambridge
Cambridgeshire
0223 324577

JUST FOR THE NIGHT
····

The head office for this dress hire enterprise is in St Albans (see page 79); however, this does not mean that the rest of the country need Cinderella at home. You too can go to the ball by contacting Just for the Night in ARUNDEL (0903 884279); BERKHAMSTED (0442 864088); CAMBERLEY (0276 28370); COLCHESTER (0206 540957); HAYWARDS HEATH (0444 440435); LICHFIELD (0543 415333); NORTHAMPTON (0604 720183); NORWICH (0603 633788); OXFORD (0865 513309); READING (0734 332372) and YORK (0904 766348).
····

THE GAP

A chain of plain and simple shops, all white and scrubbed pine, selling simple, wearable good young clothes for outdoor activities and just messing around. Thick jumpers, sweaters, jackets, tracksuits, jeans and jackets. Certainly not power dressing, but v. good quality and great fun to wear. All clothes are own label (The Gap), sizes 10 to 14. Prices are affordable, and there are excellent sales in January. Hours vary from store to store, but the Long Acre shop is open from 10.00 to 8.00 every day except Sunday when it opens from 12.00 to 7.00. Access, American Express and Visa accepted.

London Gaps:
395 Oxford Street
London W1
071 408 2400

315 Oxford Street
London W1
071 493 2091

The Plaza
Oxford Street
London W1
071 436 2861

208 Regent Street
London W1
071 434 2091

Long Acre
Covent Garden
London WC2
071 379 0779

66a High Street
Hampstead
London NW3
071 794 8112

Other Gaps:
HOME COUNTIES

38 George Street
Richmond
Surrey
081 940 8670

Unit 1
Drummond Centre
Croydon
Surrey
081 680 4504

69 High Street
Guildford
Surrey
0483 302959

THE WEST COUNTRY

Old Bond Street
Bath
Avon
0225 463132

EAST ANGLIA

Market Hll
Cambridge
Cambridgeshire
0223 324101

THE MIDLANDS

Unit 37
Victorian Centre
Nottingham
Nottinghamshire
0602 483448

THE NORTH

21–23 Church Street
Liverpool
Merseyside
051 709 0268

9–11 Blackett Bridge
Eldon Centre
Newcastle on Tyne
Tyne & Wear
091 222 1036

5–7 Spurriergate
York
Yorkshire
0904 620011

SCOTLAND

79 Argyll Street
Glasgow
041 221 0629

ISLAND GIRL
····

Chelsea Girl, the dollybird who stayed too long at the party, has grown up. Now she's River Island: the first one opened in November 1988 and another 259 are planned by September 1990. The decor is stylishly welcoming: clothes are simple shapes, good colours, versatile and wearable by women older than 16. The River Island label covers cotton jersey separates and shirts; more formal clothes go under the Charlotte Halston label. All clothes are designed in house, and much attention is paid to getting maximum style within the strict budget. Clever colours and rather dashing cut give these clothes a good start: girls and women who are saving up for Paul Costelloe can do wonders by removing the odd unnecessary trim or changing ugly buttons. Sizes 10 to 14/16, prices very good: sweeping white cotton trenchcoat for about £60.00, washed silk jumpsuit for £50.00, T-shirts for under a tenner, dashing viscose shorts around £18.00. Shoes and jewellery to complement designs, but these clothes look better dressed if you accessorize with your best. A welcome addition to the high street, neatly bridging the gap between power wannabees Next and safe and sure M&S.
····

JIGSAW

Winners of 1989's Young
Contemporary Designer of the
Year; Jigsaw's clothes are the ones
most young people want to wear.
Wonderful trousers. To people of a
certain age, the Jigsaw
Phenomenon is reminiscent of the
magnificent long lost Biba empire.
The flagship store in Kensington
High Street has the same air of
delightful club/party/clothes shop
that Biba generated. The Jigsaw
team is led by designer John
Robinson, who keeps a tight grip
on things. Great clothes, good
service, relaxed atmosphere; for
many under 30s it's the only place
to shop.

Main Jigsaws:
65 Kensington High Street
London W8
071 937 3572

and
21 Long Acre
London WC2
071 240 3855

SURREY

122 High Street
Guildford
0483 65911

46 Union Street
Kingston
081 541 4632

41 George Street
Richmond
081 940 8386

WEST COUNTRY

8 New Bond Street
Bath
Avon
0225 461613

80 Park Street
Bristol
Avon
0272 265775

66–68 The Promenade
Cheltenham
Gloucestershire
0242 525849

THE NORTH

21–23 Northgate Street
Chester
Cheshire
0244 316955

151 Grainger Street
Newcastle on Tyne
Tyne & Wear

SCOTLAND

20–21 Princes Square
Buchanan Street
Glasgow
041 204 1659

OASIS

Finally dumping their ethnic tat,
Oasis have emerged as a good
source of rather stylish,
inexpensive and unusual separates.
Wonderful one size T shirt with
unusual necklines; good knitwear
that looks more expensive than it is;
little slippy party tops and bottoms
from Monix; enormous range of
costume jewellery, especially

earrings. Generously cut clothes (10 to 14), lots of easy to wear jersey, strong colour co-ordination allows much mix and matching. Relaxing and easy on the budget.

Main Oasis:
44 St James Street
London WC2

Other Oases:
LONDON

292 Regent Street
London NW1
071 323 9317

UNIT F 15
The Plaza
Oxford Street
London W1
071 436 5185

UNIT 6
Kensington Barracks
Kensington Church Street
London W8
071 938 4019

THE SOUTH

23 Wallington Square
Wallington
Sutton
Surrey
081 773 1428

12–14 Dukes Lane
Brighton
East Sussex
0273 23492

THE MIDLANDS

33 to 35 Little Clarendon Street
Oxford OX1 2HU
Oxfordshire
0865 54859

UNIT 10
Exchange Arcade
Nottingham NG2
Nottinghamshire
0602 470880

UNIT 17
Pride Hill Centre
Shrewsbury
Shropshire SY1 1BX
0743 51981

THE NORTH

12 Bond Street Shopping Centre
Leeds
Yorkshire
0532 420464

UNIT 10
Clayton Square
Liverpoool L1 1QR
Merseyside
051 709 6862

NIGHTINGALES
····
More than just demure pintucked Victorian nighties: silky tea gowns, tiny print summer frocks, and romantic cotton evening dresses all in size 10–16 and at terrific prices: £25.00 average. Head Nightingale at 434 Finchley Road LONDON NW2 (071 435 4070); others at 169 Yorkshire Street, ROCHDALE; 3 Mount Pleasant Roundabout, COCKFOSTERS; 11 High Street, RISELEY and 13 Chesterfield Road, SHEFFIELD. Mail order from head office.
····

A NEW FASHION EPISODE

····

Episode is a spanking new shop (opened in March this year), very mellow in bleached wood and matt grey Portland stone; lots of chairs to cool out on. The clothes are as relaxed as the decor: lovely easy to wear smart casuals designed in New York. Lots of lovely sandwashed silk, cotton mix and linens in shorts, shirts, culottes, jackets, jumpsuits in uncluttered colours: barley, saffron, paprika, navy, cream, and of course black and white. Prices are good: plain cotton body in lots of assorted colours £29.00, silk pants from £49.00 calf length skirt £79.00, the quintessential white cotton parka for £99.00.

····

Episode is the brainchild of Susan Wolff, design director of S R Gent, one of the mainstays of M & S womenswear. You know you are getting style plus quality. Another Episode in Bath, and further instalments planned if all goes well.

····

Episode
9–13 Brompton Road
London SW3
071 584 7047
Open: 10.00 to 6.00 Mon. to Sat.

····

WHISTLES

Smart daywear and designer clothes gathered together by Lucille Lewin: easy wearable office clothes spiked with drama: Lolita Lempicka, Myrène de Prémonville, Georgina Godley. Easy to spend all your money here.

Main Whistles:
12–14 St Christopher's Place
London W1
071 487 4484

Other Whistles:
14 Beauchamp Place
London SW3
071 581 4830

27 Sloane Street
London SW1
071 730 8919

1 Thayer Street
London W1
071 935 7013

26 The Market
London WC2
071 379 7401

1 Kingswell Centre
Heath Street
London NW3
071 431 22395

19 Hill Street
Richmond
081 332 1646

9 High Street
Oxford
0865 728336

15 Princes Square
Glasgow
041 226 5259

Shoes

HOBBS

Extremely comfortable fashion
shoes: brogues, loafers, flatties,
boots and plain courts in the
season's colours, designed by
clever Marion Anselm. Nurses at
London's UCH swear by them.
Anselm also designs lovely easy to
wear clothes. Shoe sizes 3 to 8;
prices £30.00 plus.

Main Shop:
84 King's Road
London SW3
071 581 2914

Others:
47 South Molton Street
London W1
071 629 0750

37 Brompton Road
London SW3
071 225 2136

17, The Piazza
Covent Garden
London WC2
071 836 9168

9 and 15 High Street
Hampstead
London NW3
071 435 6969

3 The Barkers
Kensington High Street
London W8
071 937 1026

WELSH DRESSERS
····

The CARA operation is centred
on the daft, delightful demented
Italianate village of
Portmeirion. Bags of designer
input meets wonderful ethnicy
fabrics; all design from Cara
Studio in Tremadog (0776
514485) and clothes made up in
Hong Kong and India (although
local production is in the
pipeline). This year sees soft
floaty skirts and jackets in
dreamy voiles, cool formal
heavy cotton suits featuring
tight Nehru-style leggings
under the skirt, huge boxy tops
and enormous baggy pants in
bright batik, mix and match
summer separates. Also little
cotton knits appliquéd with
embroidery to echo the fabric
prints; and the occasional silk
extravaganzas. Sizes are 10 to
16, although many styles are one
size: prices average at £40.00.
····
Cara shops in Wales also at Unit
2–4 Great Darkgate Street,
ABERYSTWYTH SY23 1DE; 317
High Street, BANGOR LL57
1YA; 9 Duke Street, CARDIFF
CF11 2AY, and 96 High Street,
PORTHMADOG. Non-cymru
branches at 42 Bridge Street,
CHESTER and Unit 13,
Whiteleys, Bayswater,
LONDON. And at 15b Blenheim
Crescent, London W11 they
have their sale shop...
····

PIED A TERRE

Stylish well made very wearable shoes, mostly French design. Occasionally quietly saucy. Sizes 35 to 41; prices around £30.00 plus. Mail order and repairs. Pied a Terre account card gives you access to special preview evenings.

Basics are just as yummy, but less dressy and very reasonably priced (around £30.00 start).

Main Pieds:
19 South Molton Street
London W1
071 629 1362

Others Pieds:
14 Sloane Street
London SW1
071 235 0564

33 King's Road
London SW3
071 730 9240

5 Garrick Street
London WC2
071 836 8129

31 High Street,
Hampstead
London NW3
071 433 3858

124 Draycott Avenue
London SW3
071 225 1794

Princes Square
Buchanan Street
Glasgow
041 221 0463

PIEDS A TERRE also in Way In HARRODS and FENWICKS.

PIED A TERRE BASICS

The Plaza
Oxford Street
London W1
071 436 4137

122 King's Road
London SW3
071 823 8528

The Colonnades
Bath Street
Bath
Avon
0225 448505

23 Dukes Lane
Brighton
East Sussex
0273 204762

BERTIES

Although it is part of the mighty Sears group (they own Selfridges and other chunks of the planet), the Bertie label produces unusual offbeat styles, mostly all leather, at decent prices. Sizes 35 to 41, will also do repairs. Main Bertie at **36 South Molton Street**. Other London Bertie's at **8a Sloane Street**, **409 Oxford Street**, **118 King's Road**, **65 Hampstead High Street**, **Unit 15 Covent Garden** and **23 Long Acre**; out of town Berties at **Units 2 and 10**, **The Gardens**, Exchange Street, **Manchester**, **75 High Street Guildford** and **17a Eastgate Row, Chester**.

CLOTHES AND FABRIC CARE

••••••••••

Both investment dressing, fun wear and
'bread and butter' clothes will repay
careful maintenance to get the best out
of them. The following charts are
designed to help you both launder natural
fibres successfully and to pick your way
through the man-made fibre jungle. Also
a size chart showing UK and continental
sizes: but remember, it is a truth
universally acknowledged that one
label's 12 is another label's 14.

REVISED TEXTILE CARE LABELLING CODE

Old Symbol	New Symbol	Accompanying Wording	Washing temperature	
			Machine	Hand
⌐1̲⌐ 95°	⌐95⌐	'wash in cotton cycle/ programme' or 'wash as cotton'	very hot 95°C *normal action, rinse and spin*	hand hot
⌐2̲⌐ 60°	⌐60⌐	'wash in cotton cycle/ programme' or 'wash as cotton'	hot 60°C *normal action, rinse and spin*	hand hot
⌐4̲⌐ 50°	⌐50⌐ ▬	'wash in synthetics cycle/ programme' or 'wash as synthetics'	hand hot 50°C *reduced action, cold rinse, reduced spin or drip dry*	
⌐5̲⌐ 40°	⌐40⌐	'wash in cotton cycle/ programme' or 'wash as cotton'	warm 40°C *normal action, rinse and spin*	
⌐6̲⌐ 40°	⌐40⌐ ▬	'wash in synthetics cycle/ programme' or 'wash as synthetics'	warm 40°C *reduced action, cold rinse, reduced spin*	
⌐7̲⌐ 40°	⌐40⌐ ▬▬	'wash in wool cycle/ programme' or 'wash as wool'	warm 40°C *much reduced action, normal rinse and spin*	
⌐✋⌐	⌐✋⌐	Hand wash	See garment label	
⋈	⋈	Do not wash		

WASHING TEMPERATURES

100°C	Boil	Self explanatory
95°C	Very hot	Water heated to near boiling temperature.
60°C	Hot	Hotter than the hand can bear. The temperature of water coming from many domestic hot taps.
50°C	Hand hot	As hot as the hands can bear.
40°C	Warm	Pleasantly warm to the hand.

ic type

for white cotton and linen articles without special finishes, this process provides the most vigorous conditions. The high water temperature and maximum agitation and spinning times ensure good ·ness and stain removal.

otton, linen or viscose articles without special finishes where colours are fast at 60°C. Provides ·ous wash conditions but at a temperature which maintains fast colours.

ylon; polyester/cotton mixtures; polyester; cotton and viscose articles with special finishes; cotton/ ·ic mixtures. Reduced agitation and the lower wash temperature safeguards the finish and colour. rinsing followed by short spinning minimises creases.

d to cotton, linen and viscose articles where colours are fast at 40°C but not at 60°C. This process ·es thorough cleansing but at the lower wash temperature essential to safeguard colour fastness.

hose articles which require gentle, low temperature laundering to preserve colour and shape and ·nise creasing eg acrylics; acetate and triacetate, including mixtures with wool; polyester/wool ·s.

wool, including blankets, wool mixed with other fibres, and silk, requiring low temperature ·ing with minimum agitation. This treatment preserves colour, size and texture. Do not rub or wring.

de articles with Programme 3 60°C care label in ⌴50⌴

de articles with Programme 8 30°C care label in ⌴40⌴ or ⌴40⌴

·NIFICANCE OF THE BAR UNDERNEATH THE WASH TUB

·nce of bar ⌴⌴ denotes normal (maximum) machine action and is labelled 'wash as cotton'.

·r ⌴⌴ denotes reduced (medium) machine action and is labelled 'wash as synthetics'.

·ken bar ⌴⌴ denotes much reduced (minimum) wash action and labelled 'wash as wool'.

·ING WASH LOADS

·can mix wash labels without a bar provided you wash at the lowest temperature shown.

·can mix wash labels with and without a bar provided that you wash at the lowest temperature, you must reduce the wash action.

·es with ⌴40⌴ must be washed as wool at a much reduced wash action.

·n separately' means what it says.

BLEACHING

This symbol indicates that household (chlorine) bleach could be used. Care must be t to follow the manufacturer's instructions.

When this symbol appears on a label household bleach must *not* be used.

IRONING

The number of dots in the ironing symbol indicates the correct temperature setting – fewer the dots the cooler the iron setting.

cool   warm   hot   do not iron

DRY CLEANING

The letter in the circle refers to the solvent which may be used in the dry-cleaning pro and those using 'coin op' dry-cleaning should check that the cleaning symbol shown o label is the same as that in the instructions given on the front of the machine.

Goods normal for dry-cleaning in all solvents.

Goods normal for dry-cleaning in perchloroethylene, white spirit, Solvent 113 and So 11.

Goods normal for dry-cleaning in white spirit or Solvent 113.

Do not dry-clean.

N.B. When the circle containing P or F is underlined, do not 'coin op' clean, as this ind that these materials are sensitive to dry cleaning and require special treatment.

DRYING

Care labels may also include one or other of the following symbols recommending a particular drying method.

Tumble dry on a low heat setting.

Tumble dry on a high heat setting.

Do not tumble dry.

Where the prohibition symbol above is used, further instructions, such as 'dry flat' for k knitted garments, should be given in words.

IDENTIFYING MAN-MADE FIBRES

re Brand nes	Man-made Fibre Group	Fibre-Brand Names	Man-Made Fibre Group
el	ACETATE		
lan rtelle an lon on	ACRYLIC	Dacron Diolen Fortrel Mitrelle Quallofil Tergal Terinda Terlenka Terylene Trevira	POLYESTER
a	ELASTANE		
ex	METALLIC	Meraklon	POLYPROPYLENE
lan SEF ekalon an	MODACRYLIC (Flame retardant properties)	Arnel Tricel	TRIACETATE
on nylon trece a Nylon a Perlon ul ntesse el esse drelle brelle	NYLON (POLYAMIDE)	Danufil Danuflor Durafil Evlan Fibro Sarille Viloft	VISCOSE

e: Some items of clothing and household textiles/articles may carry a fibre content label indicating fibre group, eg acetate, nylon, instead of the brand name of the fibre.

CLOTHES SIZES

WOMEN'S SHOES

British	3	4	5	6	7	8	9
American	4.5	5.5	6.5	7.5	8.5	9.5	10.5
European	35	36	37	38	39	40	41

WOMEN'S DRESSES, COATS AND BLOUSES

British	10	12	14	16	18	20
American	8	10	12	14	16	18
French	40	42	44	46	48	50
Italian	44	46	48	50	52	54

DESIGN DIRECTORY

· · · · · · · · · ·

The Design Directory functions as an index, but includes separate listings: few shops now restrict their ranges to one clothing category, and many designers now offer the jewellery to go with the hat to go with the dress. To help you find the best of these, we supply an alphabetical listing of general shops, plus listings under accessories, hats, jewellery, knitwear, lingerie, shoes and swimwear as well as special sizes (large and small), made to measure and dress hire. There is also a listing of markets and where to find cheap chic. Finally, for aspirational purposes, there is a list of the top flight designers not included in the book. Dream on.

MAIN LISTING

*Signifies information is in the boxed section of the page

A

ABONNE
Harrow, London 81
ACADEMY SOHO
Soho, London W1 *110
ADAM'S APPLE
Woodbridge, Suffolk 75
AKIMBO
Manchester 18
RICHARD ALAN
Cork, Ireland 149
Dublin, Ireland 150
AMBERS OF AMERSHAM
Amersham, Bucks 78
AMBIANCE
Colchester, Essex 72
AMI
Gateshead, Tyne & Wear 25
Newcastle upon Tyne, Tyne & Wear 26
ANANDA
Brighton, Sussex 122
ANGEL GABRIEL
Southampton, Hants 121
ANNABELINDA
Oxford, Oxon 50
ANOKHI
London and branches 157
ARANA
Colchester, Essex *73
ASHFORD CASTLE BOUTIQUE
Cong, Ireland 151
AVOCA WEAVERS
Avoca, Co Wicklow, Ireland 148
Bath, Avon 59
Bray, Co Wicklow, Ireland 148
Bunratty, Co Clare, Ireland 149
Letterfrack, Connemara, Ireland 152
AUBERGINE
Newcastle upon Tyne, Tyne & Wear 25

B

BAMBOO
Leicester, Leics 42
BETTY BARCLAY
Manchester 18
ANNE BARNES INTERNATIONAL FASHION
Alderley Edge, Cheshire 14
ANGELA BEER
Bramhall, Greater Manchester 22
BLANCHE OF ALTRINCHAM
Altrincham, Cheshire 17
Hanley, Staffs 50
BLONDES
Glasgow, Scotland 136
BLONDIES
Abergavenny, Wales 142
BLOSSOMS
Cuckfield, Sussex 130
BLUE LEADER
Hereford, Hereford & Worcester 41
BODY BASICS
Cardiff, Wales 144
BOULES
Bristol, Avon 59
Cambridge, Cambs 70
Exeter, Devon 61
BOWLERS
Norwich, Norfolk 74
BOYD & STOREY
Soho, London W1 *110
BREATHLESS
Newcastle upon Tyne, Tyne & Wear 26
EMILY BRIGDEN
Derby, Derbys 40
BROCKLEHURST FABRICS
Macclesfield, Cheshire *16
BROWNS
Mayfair, London W1 *106
BROWN THOMAS
Dublin, Ireland 150

C

CHANTERELLE
Oxted, Surrey 83
CARA
Portmeirion, Wales and branches *163
CAMPUS
Oxford, Oxon 46
Edinburgh, Scotland 133
Glasgow, Scotland 137
CAPRICCIO
Lewes, Sussex 130
PADDY CAMPBELL
Mayfair, London W1 106
ALLY CAPELLINO
Soho, London W1 106
CATCH 22
Bath, Avon 56
CHEQUERS
Bristol, Avon 60
Southgate, London N14 97
CAROLINE CHARLES
Chelsea, London SW3 107

G

THE GAP
London W1 and
   branches 158–159
JUNIOR GAULTIER
Soho, London W1 *110
GEORGINA
Pershore, Hereford &
   Worcester 41
MADY GERRARD
Newport, Gwent,
   Wales *142
GOING DUTCH
Aberdeen, Scotland 132
GOOD HABIT
Swansea, Wales 145
MARY GRAEME
Brighton, Sussex 128, 129
JUDY GRAHAM
Cheltenham, Glos 64
Cirencester, Glos 67
ELIZABETH GRAY
Oldham, Lancs 22

H

KATHARINE
HAMNETT
London SW1 107
HARPERS
Edgware, Greater
   London 81
ERIKA HARRIS
Leeds, Yorks
ALISON HARRISON
Cheltenham, Glos 65
Leamington Spa,
   Warwicks 52
ANNABEL HARRISON
Bath, Avon 56
Oxford, Oxon 47

HARRODS
Knightsbridge, London
   SW1 86
HARVEY NICHOLS
Knightsbridge, London
   SW1 87
HELEN HAYES
Barnes, London
   SW13 118
HEWLETTS
Bradford, Yorks 30
Harrogate, Yorks 32
See also *31
HOBBY & CRACKERS
Cardiff, Wales 144
PAM HOGG
Soho, London W1 *110
HOOPERS LIMITED
Cheltenham, Glos 65
Chichester, Sussex 130
Colchester, Essex 72
Torquay, Devon 63
Tunbridge Wells,
   Kent 122
Wilmslow, Cheshire 16
HOURGLASS
Richmond, Surrey 118
MARGARET HOWELL
Chelsea, London
   SW3 107
HUDSON & HUDSON
Bristol, Avon 60
Cardiff, Wales 144
HYPER HYPER
Kensington, London
   W8 *109

I

IMAGE
Bath, Avon 57
IMAGE ITALIA
Bath, Avon 57

INTERNATIONAL
FASHIONS
Huddersfield, Yorks 33
ICHI NI SAN
Glasgow, Scotland 137
HOUSE OF ISOBEL
Birmingham, West
   Midlands 52

J

JAEGER AT
JOSEPHINE WARREN
Lymington, Hants 121
KATIE JAMES
Farnham, Surrey 82
NORMA JAMES
Corbridge,
   Northumberland 25
JANE
Cambridge, Cambs 70
Newmarket, Suffolk 75
Norwich, Norfolk 74
JANE & DADA
Mayfair, London W1 103
JENNERS
Edinburgh,
   Scotland *133
VANIA JESMOND
Swansea, Wales 146
JIGSAW
London and
   branches 160
MONICA JOHN
Cork, Ireland 149
Dublin, Ireland 151
RUBY JONES
Brighton, Sussex
JOSEPH
Chelsea, London
   SW3 108
JUNGLES
Abergavenny, Wales 142

JULES
Strawberry Hill,
London 118
JULES B
Newcastle upon Tyne,
Tyne & Wear 27

K

ALICIA KITE
Doncaster, Yorks 29
Nottingham, Notts 45
Sheffield, Yorks 36
KNIGHTSBRIDGE
Leicester, Leics 42
KOKO
Covent Garden, London
WC2 100
KRISP
Kilburn, London
NW6 97
KUMAGAI
Hampstead, London
NW3 91

L

LABELS FOR LESS
Harrogate, Yorks 32
LAURENCE CORNER
Camden, London
NW1 *92
LE MAGASIN
Brighton, Sussex 124
LETTUCE &
MULBERRY
Aberystwyth, Wales 143
LIBERTY
Brighton, Sussex 123
Mayfair, London W1 87
LITTLE BLACK DRESS
Leeds, Yorks 34
LOLIPOP
Norwich, Norfolk 74

M

MACDONALD
MACKAY
Glasgow, Scotland *139
ANDREA MACKIE
Edinburgh, Scotland 134
MADELEINE ANN
Bath, Avon 58
Solihull, West
Midlands 54
Stratford on Avon,
Warwicks 52
Worcester, Hereford &
Worcester 41
MADEMOISELLE
Beckenham, Kent 80
JOHNNY MALLE
Birmingham, West
Midlands 52
MARADIDI
Ilkley, Yorks 30
MARIANNE'S
Sunderland, Tyne &
Wear 28
THE MARINA
COLLECTION
Swansea, Wales 146
MARKS & SPENCER
Mayfair, London W1 103
MATCH
Oxford, Oxon 48
MONDI
Nottingham, Notts 46
MONK'S DORMITORY
Colchester, Essex 73
MOON
Glasgow, Scotland 138
MORSE CODE
Carmarthen, Wales 145
Swansea, Wales 146
MOUSSIE
Chelsea, London
SW3 114

THE MULBERRY
COMPANY
Mayfair, London W1 104

N

NAMES
Brighton, Sussex 124
NATALY
Brighton, Sussex 124
NETHERWOODS
York, Yorks 38
NEXT TO NOTHING
Oxford, Oxon 48
NIGHTINGALE
London NW2 and
branches *161
NOUVELLE
Oxted, Surrey 83
NOYADD RHULENS
Brecon, Wales 143

O

OASIS
London WC2 and
branches 160, 161
ALBERRE ODETTE
Notting Hill, London
W2 98
BRUCE OLDFIELD
Chelsea, London
SW3 109
OTOKIO
Cork, Ireland 149
Dublin, Ireland 152

P

PACE
Sheffield, Yorks 36

PARTNERS
Newcastle upon Tyne,
Tyne & Wear 27
PEACHES & CREAM
Newcastle upon Tyne,
Tyne & Wear 28
PERIA
Weybridge, Surrey 84
PICKETT
Mayfair, London
W1 *103
PINKY'S
Birmingham, West
Midlands 53
POLLYANNA
Barnsley, Yorks 30
POPPY
Lytham St Annes,
Lancs 24
POSH
Exeter, Devon 62
PRIMAVERA
Cambridge, Cambs 71

R

RAGGS
Cowbridge, Wales 145
RAGS
Aberdeen, Scotland 132
Brechin, Scotland 133
REACTION PREMIER
ACADEMY
Manchester 19
REBECCA
Maidenhead, Berks 77
REFLECTIONS
Nantwich, Cheshire 15
JOHN RICHMOND
Soho, London W1 *110
RIVE GAUCHE
Marlow, Bucks 79
RIZZO
Birmingham, West
Midlands 53

JOY ROBSON
Lichfield, Staffs 50
ROCHELLE
Colchester, Essex 73
ROKIT
Brighton, Sussex *123
EDINA RONAY
Chelsea, London
SW3 109
SUSAN ROOKE
Woodbridge, Suffolk 75
ROOM 7
Leeds, Yorks 35
ROSY & CO
Altrincham, Cheshire 18

S

SALUTE
Brighton, Sussex 124
SARA
Manchester 20
See also HEWLETTS
and *31
SAXS
Brighton, Sussex 124
Glasgow, Scotland 138
SEPTEMBER THREE
Birmingham, West
Midlands 54
Stratford on Avon,
Warwicks 52
SILKS
Beverley,
Humberside 23
SISTER CODY
Plymouth, Devon 63
VIVIENNE SMITH
SIMPLY CLOTHES
Bath, Avon 58
Bristol, Avon 60
Guildford, Surrey 82
Hull, Humberside 23
Leeds, Yorks 35

Nottingham, Notts 45
Sheffield, Yorks 35
Wakefield, Yorks 37
York, Yorks 38
See also *29
EMMA SOMERSET
Southport, Cheshire 24
Wilmslow, Cheshire 16
See also *19
SOMETHING SPECIAL
Stone, Staffs 51
SPANGLES
Marlborough, Wilts 67
SQUARE
Bath, Avon 57
STATUS
Tavistock, Devon 64
LISA STIRLING
Chester, Cheshire 14
Manchester 20
STRIDES
St Albans, Herts 80
SWANK
Leeds, Yorks 35
SWING
Edinburgh, Scotland 135
SYBOE
Colchester, Essex *73

T

TANNERS
Hampstead, London
NW3 92
Richmond, London 119
THIRTY NINE STEPS
Huddersfield, Yorks 33
TIZZIE D
Cheltenham, Glos 65
TOP SECRET
BOUTIQUE
Plymouth, Devon 63
TRAPEZE
Cheltenham, Glos 65

THISLEY TEXTILE
DESIGNS
Godalming, Surrey 82
TUCAN
Brighton, Sussex 127
TUMI
Oxford, Oxon 48
TUNNEL DESIGNER
CENTRE
Middlesborough,
   Cleveland 17
Newcastle upon Tyne,
   Tyne & Wear 28
TUSCANI
Stourbridge, Hereford &
   Worcester 41
21 DUKES LANE
Brighton, Sussex 125

V

VALENTINA
Leicester, Leics 42
Nottingham, Notts 46
Peterborough, Cambs 71
VERVE
Bath, Avon 58
VIEW
Hampstead, London
   NW3 92
Richmond, London 119
SARAH VIVIAN
GALLERY
Dawlish, Devon 61

W

THE WAISTCOAT
GALLERY
Mayfair, London
   W1 *105

CATHERINE WALKER
CHELSEA DESIGN
COMPANY
Chelsea, London
   SW3 109
THE WAREHOUSE
Glasgow, Scotland 139
R. WATSON HOGG
Auchterarder,
   Scotland 132
CAPTAIN OM WATTS
Mayfair, London
   W1 *107
WHISTLES
London and branches 162
WILLY'S
Exeter, Devon 62
YVETTE WINOCOUR
Glasgow, Scotland 139
HELEN WINTERSON
LIMITED
Stockport, Greater
   Manchester 22
SHIRLEY WONG
Soho, London W1 110
JANET WOOD
FASHIONS
Bath, Avon 58
Yeovil, Somerset 67
WORKERS FOR
FREEDOM
Soho, London W1 110
WORKSHOP
Richmond, London 119
WRAPS
Chelmsford, Essex 72

X

XYZ
Hampstead, London
   NW3 93

Y

JANE YOUNG
Newark, Notts 44
Nottingham, Notts 46
YOUNG IDEAS
Ashbourne, Derbys 40
SHOES AT YOUNG
IDEAS
Ashbourne, Derbys 40

Z

BASIA ZARYZKA
Chelsea, London
   SW3 *111
ZIGZAG
Altrincham, Greater
   Manchester 18
Chester, Cheshire 14
Wilmslow, Cheshire 16
Nottingham, Notts 46

ACCESSORIES

Bags, Gloves, Scarves,
Stockings, Tights

Speciality shops

ACCENT
Weybridge, Surrey 84
BACCARA
Wimbledon, London 115
BRANCHE
St John's Wood, London
   NW8 93
CARPET BAGS
Bury St Edmunds,
   Suffolk 154
DESIGN ALSO
Islington, London N1 95

INSIDE OUT
Brighton, Sussex 126
TANNERS
Hampstead, London
    NW3 92
Richmond, London 119

*Shops with good
accessory range*

BODY BASICS
Cardiff, Wales 144
EMILY BRIGDEN
Derby, Derbys 40
CATCH 22
Bath, Avon 56
DICKINS & JONES
Mayfair, London W1
DUKES
Exeter, Devon 62
FENWICKS
Mayfair, London W1 86
Newcastle upon Tyne,
    Tyne & Wear *27
JANET FITCH
Soho, London W1 104
FRED & GINGER
Enfield, Greater
    London 81
HOOPERS LIMITED
Cheltenham, Glos 65
Chichester, Sussex 130
Colchester, Essex 72
Torquay, Devon 63
Tunbridge Wells,
    Kent 122
Wilmslow, Cheshire 16
JENNERS
Edinburgh,
    Scotland *133
RUBY JONES
Brighton, Sussex
LIBERTY
Brighton, Sussex 123
Mayfair, London W1 87

MADELEINE ANN
Bath, Avon 58
Solihull, West
    Midlands 54
Stratford on Avon,
    Warwicks 52
Worcester, Hereford &
    Worcester 41
MADEMOISELLE
Beckenham, Kent 80
THE MULBERRY
COMPANY
Mayfair, London W1 104
PICKETT
Mayfair, London
    W1 *103
PRAGNELL SHOES
Cheltenham, Glos 66
REBECCA
Maidenhead, Berks 77
LISA STIRLING
Chester, Cheshire 14
Manchester 20
TUCAN
Brighton, Sussex 127
TUMI
Oxford, Oxon 48

DRESS HIRE

AMI
Newcastle upon Tyne 26
A CHANCE TO DANCE
Clapham, London
    SW11 115
ESCAPADE
Camden, London NW1
FLAPPERS
Cambridge, Cambs 70
THE FROCKERY
West Hampstead,
    London NW6 98
JUST FOR THE NIGHT
St Albans, Herts 79
Other branches 157

MACDONALD
MACKAY
Glasgow, Scotland *139
SOIREE
Cheltenham, Glos 66
20TH CENTURY FROX
Clapham, London
    SW6 116

HATS

Speciality shops

CLOTH HEADS and
SLUMSKULLS
Manchester 20
HATTERS
Hove, Sussex 126
THE HAT SHOP
Covent Garden, London
    WC2 100
Glasgow, Scotland 140
JAMES
Nottingham, Notts 45
PORCHESTER HATS
Notting Hill, London
    W2 99
JANE SMITH STRAW
HATS
London SW8 116
THAT HAT SHOP
Bristol, Avon 60
THAT HAT SHOP
Salisbury, Wilts 68
TITFERS
Bath, Avon 59
KIRSTEN
WOODWARD
Notting Hill, London
    W10 99
BASIA ZARYZKA
Chelsea, London
    SW3 *111

Shops with strong hat ranges

ACADEMY SOHO
Soho, London W1 ★110
ACCENT
Weybridge, Surrey 84
  also hat hire
AMBERS OF AMERSHAM
Amersham, Bucks 78
BAMBOO
Leicester, Leics 42
BLOSSOMS
Cuckfield, Sussex 130
DICKINS & JONES
Mayfair, London W1
DUKES
Exeter, Devon 62
FENWICKS
Mayfair, London W1 86
Newcastle upon Tyne,
  Tyne & Wear ★27
ELIZABETH GRAY
Oldham, Lancs 22

Hat hire

HOOPERS LIMITED
Cheltenham, Glos 65
Chichester, Sussex 130
Colchester, Essex 72
Torquay, Devon 63
Tunbridge Wells,
  Kent 122
Wilmslow, Cheshire 16
HOUSE OF ISOBEL
Birmingham, West
  Midlands 52
JENNERS
Edinburgh,
  Scotland ★133
RAGGS
Cowbridge, Wales 145
JANET WOOD FASHIONS
Bath, Avon 58
Yeovil, Somerset 58

JEWELLERY

All jewellery is the costume variety, unless otherwise specified

Speciality shops

DANLANN DE BAIREAD
Camden, London
  NW1 ★88
BEARDS
Cheltenham, Glos 65
BRANCHE
St John's Wood, London
  NW8 93
BUTLER & WILSON
Mayfair, London W1 111
Glasgow, Scotland 140
COBRA & BELLAMY
Mayfair, London W1 111
FFWD
Soho, London W1 ★110
JANET FITCH
Soho, London W1 104
FRONTIERS
Notting Hill, London
  W11 99
THE GREAT FROG
Soho, London W1 ★110
JESS JAMES
Soho, London W1 ★110
PENHALIGON
Covent Garden, London
  WC2 ★101
PURE FABRICATION
Soho, London W1 104
VERTU
Islington, London N1 96
GILL WING
Islington, London
  N1 ★94
JENNY WREN
Cowbridge, Wales 145

Shops with major jewellery input

ACADEMY SOHO
Soho, London W1 ★110
ACCENT
Weybridge, Surrey 54
ANANDA
Brighton, Sussex 122
BACCARA
Wimbledon, London 115
BAMBOO
Leicester, Leics 42
BLOSSOMS
Cuckfield, Sussex 130
BODY BASICS
Cardiff, Wales 144
CLICHE
Beaconsfield, Bucks 78
CLIVE & PHILIP
Brighton, Sussex 126
DESIGN ALSO
Islington, London N1 95
DICKINS & JONES
Mayfair, London W1 86
DUKES
Exeter, Devon 62
FENWICKS
Mayfair, London W1 86
Newcastle upon Tyne,
  Tyne & Wear ★27
FRED & GINGER
Enfield, Greater
  London 81
GOING DUTCH
Aberdeen, Scotland 132
HOOPERS LIMITED
Cheltenham, Glos 65
Chichester, Sussex 130
Colchester, Essex 72
Torquay, Devon 63
Tunbridge Wells,
  Kent 122
Wilmslow, Cheshire 16

ALISON HARRISON
Cheltenham, Glos 65
Leamington Spa,
     Warwicks 52
ANNABEL HARRISON
Bath, Avon 56
Oxford, Oxon 47
HOBBY & CRACKERS
Cardiff, Wales 144
INSIDE OUT
Brighton, Sussex 126
JENNERS
Edinburgh,
     Scotland *133
RUBY JONES
Brighton, Sussex 126
JANE
Cambridge, Cambs 70
Newmarket, Suffolk 75
Norwich, Norfolk 74
KNIGHTSBRIDGE
Leicester, Leics 42
LIBERTY
Brighton, Sussex 123
Mayfair, London W1 87
PRAGNELL SHOES
Cheltenham, Glos 66
RAGGS
Cowbridge, Wales 145
REBECCA
Maidenhead, Berks 77
ROOM 7
Leeds, Yorks 35
TANNERS
Hampstead, London
     NW3 92
Richmond, London 119
TUCAN
Brighton, Sussex 127
TUMI
Oxford, Oxon 48

KNITWEAR

Speciality shops

BERK
Mayfair, W1 *103
BEATRICE BELLINI
HAND KNITS
Pimlico, London
     SW1 114
CLOTHES RAIL
Brighton, Sussex 127
MELINDA COSS
Islington, London N1 96
COTSWOLD
WOOLLENS
Cheltenham and
     branches 155
S FISHER
Mayfair, London
     W1 *103
MARION FOALE
Mayfair, London W1 112
HYNE & EAMES
Edinburgh, Scotland 135
MOUSSIE
Chelsea, London
     SW3 114
MUIR & OSBORNE
Camden, London
     NW1 89
NOTHING
Oxford, Oxon 48
N PEAL
Mayfair, London
     W1 *103
PENNY PLAIN
Newcastle upon Tyne,
     Tyne & Wear 154
PICKETT
Mayfair, London
     W1 *103
BELINDA
RUSHWORTH-LUND
Falmouth, Cornwall 61
THE SWEATER SHOP
Clitheroe,*
     Lancashire 24

WESTAWAY &
WESTAWAY
Bloomsbury, London
     WC1 101

*Shops with major
knitwear ranges*

COPPELIA
Lymington, Hants 121
THE DESIGN CENTRE
Dublin, Ireland 150
DICKINS & JONES
Mayfair, London W1
DUKES
Exeter, Devon 62
DUO
Hampstead, London
     NW3 90
FENWICKS
Mayfair, London W1 86
Newcastle upon Tyne,
     Tyne & Wear *27
GINGER
Leamington Spa,
     Warwicks 51
HOOPERS LIMITED
Cheltenham, Glos 65
Chichester, Sussex 130
Colchester, Essex 72
Torquay, Devon 63
Tunbridge Wells,
     Kent 122
Wilmslow, Cheshire 16
JANE & DADA
Mayfair, London W1 103
JENNERS
Edinburgh,
     Scotland *133
MARKS & SPENCER
Mayfair, London W1 103
RAGS
Aberdeen, Scotland 132
Brechin, Scotland 133

EDINA RONAY
Chelsea, London
  SW3 109
ROOM 7
Leeds, Yorks 35
SARAH VIVIAN
GALLERY
Dawlish, Devon 61
R WATSON HOGG
Auchterarder,
  Scotland 132

LEATHER

THE MULBERRY
COMPANY
Mayfair, London W1 104
PERIA
Weybridge, Surrey 84

LINGERIE & NIGHTWEAR

Speciality shops

DIANNE ADAMS
Leicester, Leics 43
BRIEF ENCOUNTER
Glasgow, Scotland 140
CHANTILLY
Chester, Cheshire 14
COURTNEY
Mayfair, London W1 112
ENCHANTE
Beaconsfield, Bucks 79
FEMME
Manchester 21
MARY GRAEME
Brighton, Sussex 128, 129
LINGERS
York, Yorks 38
PEACHES & CREAM
Newcastle upon Tyne,
  Tyne & Wear 28

JANET REGER
Chelsea, London
  SW3 112
RIGBY & PELLER
Knightsbridge, London
  SW3 *113
SARATOGA
Oxford, Oxon 49
SHE
Blackheath, London
  SE3 117
TEMPTATIONS
Weybridge, Surrey 84
Wimbledon, London 116

Shops with strong lingerie input

AMBERS OF
AMERSHAM
Amersham, Bucks 78
EMILY BRIGDEN
Derby, Derbys 40
DESIGN ALSO
Islington, London N1 95
DICKINS & JONES
Mayfair, London W1
DUKES
Exeter, Devon 62
FENWICKS
Mayfair, London W1 86
Newcastle upon Tyne,
  Tyne & Wear *27
HOOPERS LIMITED
Cheltenham, Glos 65
Chichester, Sussex 130
Colchester, Essex 72
Torquay, Devon 63
Tunbridge Wells,
  Kent 122
Wilmslow, Cheshire 16
JENNERS
Edinburgh,
  Scotland *133

KATIE JAMES
Farnham, Surrey 82
LIBERTY
Brighton, Sussex 123
Mayfair, London W1 87
MARKS & SPENCER
Mayfair, London W1 103
NIGHTINGALE
London NW2 and
  branches *161
TUSCANI
Stourbridge, Hereford &
  Worcester 41
WRAPS
Chelmsford, Essex 72

MADE-TO-MEASURE

Speciality services

DEBORAH AUGIER
St Albans, Herts 80
ANNABELINDA
Oxford, Oxon 50
MELINDA COSS
Islington, London N1 96
COCKTAIL
Islington, London N1 96
THE DESIGN STUDIO
Brighton, Sussex 128
THE DRESSING ROOM
Manchester 21
EBENEZER MISSION
Highgate, London N6
ONE OF GHILLIES
Cowbridge, Wales 154
BELINDA
RUSHWORTH-LUND
Falmouth, Cornwall 61
21 DUKES LANE
Brighton, Sussex 125

VERVE
Bath, Avon 58
THE WENDY HOUSE
Cheltenham, Glos 66

Shops where made-to-measure possible

AMBERS OF
AMERSHAM
Amersham, Bucks 78
ANNIE'S
London N1 95

PARTY & EVENING DRESS

AMBERS OF
AMERSHAM
Amersham, Bucks 78
ANNABELINDA
Oxford, Oxon 50
ANNIE'S
London N1 95
EMILY BRIGDEN
Derby, Derbys 40
A CHANCE TO DANCE
Clapham, London
 SW11 115
CHANTERELLE
Oxted, Surrey 83
COCKTAIL
Islington, London N1 96
CONCEPT
Louth, Lincs 44
ANGEL GABRIEL
Southampton, Hants 121
DICKINS & JONES
Mayfair, London W1 86
THE DRESSING ROOM
Manchester 21
DROOPY & BROWNS
Bath, Avon 56

Edinburgh 139
Covent Garden,
 London 180
York, Yorks 37
DUKES
Exeter, Devon 62
FENWICKS
Mayfair, London W1 86
Newcastle upon Tyne,
 Tyne & Wear ★27
FLAPPERS
Cambridge, Cambs 70
THE FROCKERY
West Hampstead,
 London NW6 98
HOBBY & CRACKERS
Cardiff, Wales 144
HOOPERS LIMITED
Cheltenham, Glos 65
Chichester, Sussex 130
Colchester, Essex 72
Torquay, Devon 63
Tunbridge Wells,
 Kent 122
Wilmslow, Cheshire 16
HOUSE OF ISOBEL
Birmingham, West
 Midlands 52
INTERNATIONAL
FASHIONS
Huddersfield, Yorks 33
NORMA JAMES
Corbridge,
 Northumberland 25
JANE
Cambridge, Cambs 70
Newmarket, Suffolk 75
Norwich, Norfolk 74
JENNERS
Edinburgh,
 Scotland ★133
JUST FOR THE NIGHT
St Albans, Herts 79
Other branches 157

NETHERWOODS
York, Yorks 38
REBECCA
Maidenhead, Berks 77
VIVIENNE SMITH
SIMPLY CLOTHES
Bath, Avon 58
Bristol, Avon 60
Guildford, Surrey 82
Hull, Humberside 23
Leeds, York 35
Nottingham, Notts 45
Sheffield, Yorks 35
Wakefield, Yorks 37
York, Yorks 38
See also ★29
SOIREE
Cheltenham, Glos 66
TIZZIE D
Cheltenham, Glos 65
TOP SECRET
BOUTIQUE
Plymouth, Devon 63
VERVE
Bath, Avon 58
SARAH VIVIAN
GALLERY
Dawlish, Devon 61
R WATSON HOGG
Auchterarder,
 Scotland 132
THE WENDY HOUSE
Cheltenham, Glos 66

PERIOD & ANTIQUE CLOTHES

ANNIE'S
London N1 95
CORNUCOPIA
Pimlico, London
 SW1

FLAPPERS
Cambridge, Cambs 70
LEOPARD
Brighton, Sussex 128
WARDROBE
Brighton, Sussex 128

SHOES

Speciality shops

ACCENT
Weybridge, Surrey 84
ANELLO & DAVIDE
London WC2 101
BERTIES
London & branches 164
BLOSSOMS
Cuckfield, Sussex 130
CABOODLE
Colchester, Essex *73
CIEL
Beverley,
  Humberside 23
CINZIA
Kilburn, London
  NW6 97
CORNICHE
Kenilworth,
  Warwicks 51
CRISPINS
Mayfair, London W1 105
Manchester 21
MARY GRAEME
Brighton, Sussex 128, 129
HOBBS
London and branches 163
EMMA HOPE
Clerkenwell, London
  EC1 112
JUNE JOHNSTON
Edinburgh, Scotland 135

STEPHANIE KELIAN
Chelsea, London
  SW1 113
JESSICA MOK
Clerkenwell, London
  EC1 113
PANACHE
Sheffield, Yorks 36
PERIA
Weybridge, Surrey 84
PIED A TERRE
London and branches 164
PLUMLINE
Covent Garden, London
  WC2 102
PRAGNELL SHOES
Cheltenham, Glos 66
RAFFINEE
Salisbury, Wilts 68
**SHOES AT YOUNG
IDEAS**
Ashbourne, Derbys 40
YOUNG IDEAS
Sheffield, Yorks 36

*Shops with large shoe
ranges*

**AMBERS OF
AMERSHAM**
Amersham, Bucks 78
BLUE LEADER
Hereford, Hereford &
  Worcester 41
EMILY BRIGDEN
Derby, Derbys 40
CLICHE
Beaconsfield, Bucks 78
COPPELIA
Lymington, Hants 121
DICKINS & JONES
Mayfair, London W1
DUKES
Exeter, Devon 62

FENWICKS
Mayfair, London W1 86
Newcastle upon Tyne,
  Tyne & Wear *27
FORM
Brighton, Sussex 123
HARPERS
Edgware, Greater
  London 81
HOOPERS LIMITED
Cheltenham, Glos 65
Chichester, Sussex 130
Colchester, Essex 72
Torquay, Devon 63
Tunbridge Wells,
  Kent 122
Wilmslow, Cheshire 16
JENNERS
Edinburgh,
  Scotland *133
JUNGLES
Abergavenny, Wales 142
NOYADD RHULENS
Brecon, Wales 143
SUSAN ROOKE
Woodbridge, Suffolk 75
TANNERS
Hampstead, London
  NW3 92
Richmond, London 119
**SARAH VIVIAN
GALLERY**
Dawlish, Devon 61

SPECIAL SIZES

Speciality shops

BASE
Rushka Murganovic
Covent Garden, London
  WC2 102
Parson's Green, London
  SW6 116

CLASSIC PLUS
Salisbury, Wiltshire 68
OPINIONS
Canterbury, Kent 122
Brighton, Sussex 129
Guildford, Surrey 83
KEN SMITH DESIGNS
Mayfair, London W1 105

*Shops with a good
range of larger sizes*

**AMBERS OF
AMERSHAM**
Amersham, Bucks 78
LS DEFTY
Sunderland, Tyne &
Wear 28
DICKINS & JONES
Mayfair, London W1
DUKES
Exeter, Devon 62
FENWICKS
Mayfair, London W1 86
Newcastle upon Tyne,
Tyne & Wear *27
THE EXTRA INCH
Edinburgh, Scotland 136
HEWLETTS
Bradford, Yorks 30
HOOPERS LIMITED
Cheltenham, Glos 65
Chichester, Sussex 130
Colchester, Essex 72
Torquay, Devon 63
Tunbridge Wells,
Kent 122
Wilmslow, Cheshire 16
**JAEGER AT
JOSEPHINE WARREN**
Lymington, Hants 121
JENNERS
Edinburgh,
Scotland *133

POPPY
Lytham St Annes,
Lancs 24
PRIMAVERA
Cambridge, Cambs 71
**HELEN WINTERSON
LIMITED**
Stockport, Greater
Manchester 22

*Shops with a good
range of small sizes
(6 and 8)*

CATCH 22
Bath, Avon 56
CLICHE
Beaconsfield, Bucks 78
HARPERS
Edgware, Greater
London 81
ERIKA HARRIS
Leeds, Yorks 34
**JAEGER AT
JOSEPHINE
WARREN**
Lymington, Hants 121
NORMA JAMES
Corbridge,
Northumberland 25
JANE
Newmarket, Suffolk 75
ANDREA MACKIE
Edinburgh, Scotland 134

SWIMWEAR

ADAM'S APPLE
Woodbridge, Suffolk 75
DIANNE ADAMS
Leicester, Leics 43
**AMBERS OF
AMERSHAM**
Amersham, Bucks 78

BREATHLESS
Newcastle upon Tyne,
Tyne & Wear 26
BRIEF ENCOUNTER
Glasgow, Scotland 140
CATCH 22
Bath, Avon 56
CHANTILLY
Chester, Cheshire 14
CONCEPT
Louth, Lincs 44
COPPELIA
Lymington, Hants 121
DICKINS & JONES
Mayfair, London W1 86
DUKES
Exeter, Devon 62
DUO
Hampstead, London
NW3 90
ENCHANTE
Beaconsfield, Bucks 79
FENWICKS
Mayfair, London W1 86
Newcastle upon Tyne,
Tyne & Wear *27
GINGER
Leamington Spa,
Warwicks 51
GOOD HABIT
Swansea, Wales 145
MARY GRAEME
Brighton, Sussex 128, 129
HOOPERS LIMITED
Cheltenham, Glos 65
Chichester, Sussex 130
Colchester, Essex 72
Torquay, Devon 63
Tunbridge Wells,
Kent 122
Wilmslow, Cheshire 16
KATE JAMES
Farnham, Surrey 82
JENNERS
Edinburgh,
Scotland *133

MADEMOISELLE
Beckenham, Kent 80
NOUVELLE
Oxted, Surrey 83
ONE OF GHILLIES
Cowbridge, Wales 154
PEACHES & CREAM
Newcastle upon Tyne,
   Tyne & Wear 28
ROSY & CO
Altrincham, Cheshire 18
SARATOGA
Oxford, Oxon 49
SHE
Blackheath, London
   SE3 117
TEMPTATIONS
Weybridge, Surrey 84
Wimbledon, London 116

MAIL ORDER

As well as the shops listed
in the Mail Order Section
(pages 154 and 155), a few
shops undertake mail order
or will post clothes to you
if you telephone and
describe them

AMBERS OF
AMERSHAM
Amersham, Bucks 78
DANLANN DE
BAIREAD
Camden, London
   NW1 *88
ANNE BARNES
INTERNATIONAL
FASHION
Alderley Edge,
   Cheshire 14
PAUL COSTELLOE
Amersham, Bucks 77

KEN SMITH DESIGNS
Mayfair, London W1 105
VIEW
Hampstead, London
   NW3 92
Richmond, London 119

CHEAP CHIC

MARKETS

THE BARRAS
Glasgow 140
CAMBRIDGE
Cambridge 70
CAMDEN LOCK
London N1 89
GREENWICH
London SE10 117
LEICESTER
Leicester 43
PICCADILLY
London W1 104
PORTOBELLO
London W2 98
RAG MARKET
Birmingham 53

DESIGN AT A
DISCOUNT

BURLEY SALE 44
CHELSEA DESIGNER
SALE 108
DESIGNS
Hampstead, London
   NW3 90
DISCONNECTED
Leeds, Yorks 34
LABELS FOR LESS
Harrogate, Yorks 32
NAMES
Brighton, Sussex 124

DESIGNER
SHOPPING

Where to find the heavy
brigade and some of the
shops that purvey their
clothes

Designer's Own
Shops

HARDY AMIES
14 Savile Row
London W1
071 734 2436
GIORGIO ARMANI
178 Sloane Street
London SW1
071 235 6232
Armani and Mani from here
EMPORIO ARMANI
191 Brompton Road
London SW3
071 823 8818
BELLVILLE SASSOON
73 Pavilion Road
London SW3
071 235 3087
MANOLO BLAHNIK
49 to 51 Old Church
Street London SW3
071 352 8622
DONALD CAMPBELL
8 William Street
London SW1
071 235 3332
CARTIER LTD
175 New Bond Street
London W1
071 493 6962
CHANEL
26 Old Bond Street
London W1
071 493 5040

31 Sloane Street
London SW3
071 235 6631
ROBERT CLERGERIE
67 Wigmore Street
London W1
071 935 3601
THE COACH STORE
8 Sloane Street
London SW1
071 235 1507
**COMME DES
GARCONS**
59 Brook Street
London W1
071 493 1230
also in Ichi Ni San, Glasgow
JASPER CONRAN
303 Brompton Road
London SW3
071 823 9314
THE EMANUEL SHOP
10 Beauchamp Place
London SW3
071 584 4997
FENDI
37 Sloane Street
London SW1
071 235 9966
GIANFRANCO FERRE
23 Brook Street
London W1
071 499 7348
MAUD FRIZON
31 Old Bond Street
London W1
071 493 5989
GIVENCHY
153 New Bond Street
London W1
071 495 7141
GUCCI
27 Old Bond Street
London W1
071 629 2716

KENZO
268 Brompton Road
London SW3
071 225 1354
27 Brook Street
London W1
071 629 6077
17 Sloane Street
London SW3
071 235 1991
ROLAND KLEIN
7 to 9 Tryon Street
London SW3
071 823 9179
KARL LAGERFELD
173 New Bond Street
London W1
071 493 6277
GUY LAROCHE
45 Old Bond Street
London W1
071 493 2043
**POLO RALPH
LAUREN**
143 New Bond Street
London W1
071 491 4967
JOHNNY MOKE
396 Kings Road
London SW10
071 351 2232
**JEAN AND MARTIN
PALLANT**
19 Motcomb Street
London SW1
071 259 6046
ANTHONY PRICE
34 Brook Street
London W1
071 629 5262
ZANDRA RHODES
14a Grafton Street
London W1
071 499 3596

FRATELLI ROSSETTI
177 New Bond Street
London W1
071 491 7066
196 Sloane Street
London SW1
071 259 6397
**YVES SAINT
LAURENT**
113 New Bond Street
London W1
071 493 1800
135 New Bond Street
London W1
071 493 0405
33 Sloane Street
London SW1
071 235 6706
DAVID SHILLING
44 Chiltern Street
London W1
071 935 8473
PHILIP SOMERVILLE
11 Blenheim Street,
London W1
071 629 4442
VALENTINO
160 New Bond Street
London W1
071 493 2698
173–174 Sloane Street
London SW1
071 235 5855
GIANNI VERSACE
92 Brompton Road
London SW3
071 225 0515
**VIVIENNE
WESTWOOD**
6 Davies Street
London W1
071 629 3757
430 Kings Road
London SW10
071 350 6551

Shops

A LA MODE
36 Hans Crescent
London SW1
071 584 2133
AGNES B
111 Fulham Road
London SW3
071 225 3477
CELINE
28 New Bond Street
London W1
071 493 9000
27 Brompton Road
London SW3
071 589 0053
FEATHERS
40 Hans Crescent
London W1
071 589 0356
FRANKA
11 Dover Street
London W1
071 499 4813
GALLERY 28
28 Brook Street
London W1
071 408 0329
ANOUSKA HEMPEL
2 Pond Place
London SW3
071 589 4191
JULIA
12 Grafton Street
London W1
071 629 8587
L'OR NOIR
21 Duke Street
London W1
071 487 5295
WARDROBE
17 Chiltern Street
London W1
071 935 4086

ACKNOWLEDGEMENTS

Ebury Press would like to thank the following people for their great help on this project;

Daphne Bailey, Bee Gee, Annie Blackburn, Caroline Buckland, Nikki Clarke, Eljay Crompton, Jan Croot, Susie Dakers, Penny Doubleday, Annabel Else, Susannah Fish, Geri Gibbons, Elsa Godfrey, Freddy Godfrey-Smythe, Emma-Lee Gow, Christine Harrop, Pip Hutchinson, Rebecca Knight, Jane McCausland, Mabs MacIntyre, Anne Matthews, Anne-Marie Pugh, Belinda Sarcissian, Jessica Scott-Forbes, Susanna Tee, Shirley Willis, Caroline Wood, Jeni Wright.

Birmingham Post and Birmingham Mail, Bradford Telegraph and Argus, Caernarvon Herald, Hull Daily Mail, Lancashire Evening Telegraph, Leicester Mercury, Newcastle Chronicle, The Scotsman, Scotland on Sunday, South Wales Evening Post, Sunderland Echo, Western Morning News, Wales on Sunday, Yorkshire Post.

SEE HOW PEACHY ARCHER'S IS FOR YOURSELF

TO RECEIVE A FREE MINIATURE, COMPLETE THIS FORM AND
SEND IT TO: ARCHER'S MINIATURE OFFER (GCG), PO BOX 581
BIRMINGHAM B6 7ER.

NAME_____

ADDRESS_____

_____

_____ POST CODE_____

PLEASE ALLOW 28 DAYS FOR DELIVERY.

ARCHER'S GOOD CLOTHES GUIDE

If you have a favourite fashion shop that sells great clothes – daily working clothes, party dresses, high fashion, special sizes, knitwear, lingerie, shoes, hats and accessories – takes good care of its customers, and is a pleasure to shop in, why not let us know? You can nominate as many shops as you like. Fill in the form below and send it to:

Archer's Good Clothes Guide
Ebury Press
Random Century House
20 Vauxhall Bridge Road
London SW1V 2SA

I would like to nominate the following shop(s) for the next Archer's Good Clothes Guide:

NAME OF SHOP:..

ADDRESS: ....

....

....

TELEPHONE: ....

OPEN:...

CREDIT CARDS:..

BRANCHES, IF ANY:...

....

....

WHAT CLOTHES DO THEY SELL?:...

....

HOW WOULD YOU DESCRIBE THE DECOR AND ATMOSPHERE?: ....

....

QUALITY OF SERVICE: ....

ANY FURTHER COMMENTS: ....

....

....

....

....

....

....

Your title and name:..

....

Your address:..

....

....

Signature: ....